Book of Humour

Compiled by Rewa Mirpuri

CW01080422

PUBLISHED BY THE
INTERNATIONAL SERVICE COMMITTEE OF
THE ROTARY CLUB OF SINGAPORE
TEL:(65) 7372504, FAX:(65) 7328535

ISBN NO. 981-00-3548-9

Cartoon illustrations through the courtesy of DNC Advertising (Singapore) Pte Ltd

Published by The Rotary Club of Singapore
Tel: (65) 7372504, Fax: (65) 7328535

Printed in Singapore at Bradford Press

First published in June 1992

First Reprint	- July 1992
Second Reprint	- August 1992
Third Reprint	- October 1992
Fourth Reprint	- December 1992
Fifth Reprint	- May 1993
Sixth Reprint	- August 1993
Seventh Reprint	- December 1993 (Revised Edition)
Eighth Reprint	- April 1994
Nineth Reprint	- June 1994
Tenth Reprint	- September 1994
Eleventh Reprint	- January 1995
Twelfth Reprint	- July 1995
Thirteenth Reprint	- October 1995
Fourteenth Reprint	- January 1996 (Revised Edition)
Fifteenth Reprint	- September 1996

Printed in Singapore at Bradford Press

Gloria Chan
Charter President

FOREWORD

While you laugh when reading the "Book of Humour", it makes a difference to your mood, lightening the burden of your day and also making a difference to those who will benefit from the services provided by the Rotary Club of Queensway in District 3450. The net profit from the sale of this book goes directly into the Rotary Club of Queensway Community Services Fund which is committed to a number of community projects for the new generation, including health, education and better environment. For example, one of our current projects is the "Prevention of Hepatitis B" in China, which immunizes babies and children to 6 years of age.

At the initiative of the Club's Vice-President Bob Schroeder and the Fund-Raising Committee, Rotarians in Queensway have shown their full support and unity with the printing and marketing of this book. If the humour, irony and insights within the book serves as a mirror of life for you and if you think that our causes for doing something to balance the unfortunate side of life are worthwhile, then please join us in achieving our targets by having a laugh and helping the needy through the distribution of this book!

Gloria K.P. Chan
Charter President
January 1997

Preface

You have not only bought yourself some pleasant and entertaining reading but have also helped to bring sunshine to the poor. The total proceeds from the sale of this book will be donated to various charitable projects. Thank you for your contribution to a good cause.

Having shared many jokes and anecdotes through the Club's various occasions of fellowship I was encouraged by many Rotarians to compile a book of jokes. This led me to consult my collection of the funniest and most memorable jokes which I have fed into my computer over the past 12 years. This is a hobby very dear to my heart and I am delighted that it can be put to good use.

I am sure you will enjoy reading these jokes as much as I have enjoyed compiling them. Just open and read any page at random. If you don't at least chuckle, let me know and I will consult my psychiatrist!

Happy reading with laughter

REWA

Acknowledgement

This publication is the result of the support and cooperation of the Rotarians of the Rotary Club of Queensway in Hong Kong especially the President (1996-97) Rotarian Amy Lau and members of the Board of Directors who provided significant encouragement at every stage.

The compiler wishes to acknowledge the contributions of Rotarians Thor Ramstetter, Bill Thomas, Mohan Vaswani, Morris Mathias and John Kedzierski and the other members of the Rotary Club of Singapore for making the project a success.

Contents

> Laughter is the sun that drives winter from the human face
>
> — Victor Hugo

Please consume this book in the light-hearted spirit it was compiled, and not as "facts of Life". These jokes were compiled to evoke laughter - for a good cause. Censoring jokes that might have offended doctors, husbands, wives and mothers-in-law, etc. would have resulted in no book at all! Thank you!

Marriage

When a man holds a woman's hand - before marriage it is love; after marriage it is self defence.

Marriage is a three-ring affair: first comes the engagement ring; then comes the wedding ring; then comes the suffering.

Marriage is a thing which puts a ring on a woman's finger and two rings under the man's eyes.

Marriage is Love. Love is blind. Therefore marriage is an institution for the blind.

A marriage certificate is just another name for a work permit.

Marriage is very much like a violin: after the sweet music is over, the strings are still attached.

Marriage is like a lottery. Except in a lottery, at least you have a chance.

Man is incomplete until he is married. Then he is really finished.

Marriage is a union. It is a union of souls, a union of hearts, a union of minds and a union of thoughts. But soon you'll have to pay those union dues.

Getting married is very much like going to a continental restaurant with friends. You order what you want, then when you see what the other fellow has, you wish you had ordered that.

A wedding ring is very much like a tourniquet. It prevents your circulation.

❖

Marriage is just like a box of chocolates. You have to buy the whole box just to get one little piece.

❖

It's true; all men are born free and equal - but some of them get married.

If you say that all men are fools, it's not true. Some are bachelors.

They say, "Marriage is a Bed of Roses". Yes, this is true. Except that the blooms have been plucked!!

At the cocktail party, one woman said to another, "Aren't you wearing your wedding ring on the wrong finger?" The other replied, "Yes I am, I married the wrong man."

There was this man who muttered a few words in the church and found himself married. A year later he muttered a few words in his sleep and found himself divorced.

Marriage is wonderful. If you see a bachelor you will find he has no buttons on his shirt. But if you see a married man.... you will find he has no shirt.

Marriage is a wonderful game. It's the only game where two can play and both can win.

❖

A happy marriage is a matter of give and take; the husband gives and the wife takes.

❖

Marriage is an institution in which a man loses his bachelor's degree and the woman gets her master's.

❖

A little boy asked his father, "Daddy, how much does it cost to get married?" And the father replied, "I don't know, son, I'm still paying for it."

❖

<u>Young son:</u> Is it true, Dad, I heard that in some parts of Africa a man doesn't know his wife until he marries her?
<u>Dad:</u> That happens in most countries, son.

❖

Then there was a man who said, "I never knew what real happiness was until I got married; and then it was too late."

❖

Bachelors may not have better halves but they certainly have better quarters.

Marriage is lots of fun. It's the living together that causes all the problems.

A bachelor is a man who has been crossed in love; a married man is one who has been double crossed.

"Is it true that matches are made in heaven? If so why do they cost only ten cents a box ?"

It needs two to make a marriage: a bride and an anxious mother.

They say, "Silence is Golden." - This is why most of the married men are prosperous.

When a man asks for a girl's hand in marriage, he doesn't realize that it includes the thumb under which he will ultimately be.

It is said, "Love is Blind." That's true, but marriage is an eye-opener.

❖

Love is one long sweet dream, and marriage is the alarm clock.

❖

It has been found that love makes time pass and time makes love pass.

❖

Marriage is not a word - it is a sentence - a life sentence.

❖

It's not true to say that married men live longer than unmarried men - it just seems longer.

❖

A lecturer delivering a talk on the demoralizing effect of legal separation said, "Love is a quest; the proposal a request; the giving in marriage a bequest; the actual marriage, a conquest."
"What is divorce?" a voice from back asked.
Swift as lightning came the reply, "Ah, that's the inquest."

❖

When a newly married man looks happy we know why. But when a ten-year married man looks happy - we wonder why.

❖

It is better to have loved and lost than to be married and bossed.

❖

It's nice to be married - to be able to relax, sit on the couch with a glass of beer in your hand and all night...watch your wife's favourite programmes.

❖

When I took the marriage vows I was told that I would go through thick and thin. I didn't realize that I would also have to go through thin and fat.

❖

Marriage is a big gamble for a man. But for a woman, marriage is no gamble. It's a calculated risk.

❖

Husbands generally grow very tender after ten years of marriage. However, any chunk of meat gets tender if you put it in hot water long enough.

❖

Of Husbands and Wives

Nowadays when a wife gives a helping hand to her husband, it's usually to tie his apron.

Woman is unpredictable. Before marriage she expects a man; after marriage she suspects him; and after death she respects him.

There was this guy who told his woman that he loved her so much that he would go through hell for her. They got married - and now he is going through hell.

If a man stays away from his wife for 7 years, the law presumes the separation to have killed him; yet judging by our daily experience it might well prolong his life.

Married life changes over time. In the first year of marriage, the man speaks and the woman listens. In the second year, the woman speaks and the man listens. In the third year, they both speak and the neighbours listen.

A married man complained: "I cannot understand marriage. If I come home early my wife thinks I am after something; and if I come home late she thinks I have had it."

❖

Wife - the letters stand for Worries Inherited For Eternity.

❖

It doesn't matter how often a married man changes his job, he still ends up with the same boss.

❖

A widow is a woman who stayed with her husband so long that he died.

❖

A woman inserted an ad in the classifieds: "Husband wanted". Next day she received a hundred letters. They all said the same thing: "You can have mine."

❖

After a quarrel, a wife said to her husband, "You know, I was a fool when I married you." And the husband replied, "Yes dear, but I was in love and didn't notice it."

❖

One man finds happiness when he finds a wife; another when he loses her.

How about this for an ideal well-matched married couple? He snores and she is deaf.

It's easy to tell if a man is married or not. Just watch him drive a car with a woman sitting beside him. If both his hands are on the wheel, you can be sure he is married.

When a man opens the door of his car for his wife, you can be sure of one thing: either the car is new or the wife.

I overheard a man complain, "Last week my luck was terrible, the chauffeur ran off without my wife."

I know a very happy married couple. They are madly in love. He with the maid and she with the doctor.

Have you heard of a new gadget that does all the household work for a woman? It's called a husband.

<u>Wife to husband:</u> George, you were talking in your sleep last night.

<u>George:</u> Oh, was I? Sorry to have interrupted you.

❖

A perfect wife is one who helps her husband with the dishes.

❖

A woman was telling her friend, "It is I who made my husband a millionaire."

"And what was he before you married him?" asked her friend.

The woman replied, "A multi - millionaire."

❖

During a heated argument between a husband and wife, the husband shouted, "You talk like an idiot." The wife replied, "I have to, so that you can understand me."

❖

A man received a letter from some kidnappers. The letter said, "If you don't promise to send us $5000/-, we promise you we will kidnap your wife." The poor man wrote back, "I am afraid I can't keep my promise but I hope you will keep yours."

❖

Here's a definition of a happily married couple : a husband out with another man's wife.

"What's the matter? You look depressed."
"I'm having trouble with my wife."
"What happened?"
"She said she wasn't going to speak to me for 30 days."
"But that ought to make you happy."
"It did, but today is the last day."

This man was telling his friends, "My wife worships me."
"Really?" they asked.
"Yes," he replied, "she places burnt offerings in front of me everyday".

Seeing so many books on the shelf, the guest asked the hostess, "Is your husband a book worm?" "No," replied the hostess, "just an ordinary one."

During a quarrel, the husband pointed a donkey out to his wife and said, "There goes your relative." The wife replied, "Yes, by marriage."

Two men met - one said, "My wife is an angel."
The other man replied, "You're lucky; mine is still alive."

A woman was boasting to her friend, "You know, I am a well known collector of antiques."
Her friend replied, "Yes I know, I have seen your husband."

Then there was this magician who took a saw and cut his wife in half because she said she wanted a separation.

A man wanted to go to Bangkok alone, so he told his wife, "Darling, my doctor says that I need a change of climate."
His wife replied, "That's fine. According to the weather report it's coming tomorrow."

There was this friend of mine who was boasting, "You know, I am the master. In my house I run things." How right he was, because when I went to his house, he was running - the washing machine, the vacuum cleaner and the lawn mower.

❖

After receiving a modest birthday gift, a wife was boasting to her husband, "My father always chooses something expensive when he gives a present."
The husband replied, "Yes dear, so I discovered when he gave you away."

Two friends met at the bar and one asked the other: "Do you ever speak to your wife when making love?"
His friend replied: "Only if she phones."

A man seeing his friend rushing with a worried look on his face asked, "Why are you in such a hurry?"
"I'm on my way to the doctor," said his friend, "I don't like the look of my wife."
"Oh!" said the man, "then I'll come with you... I hate the sight of mine too!"

Absence makes the heart grow fonder, but only before marriage. A wife phoned her husband from a health resort and sweetly pleaded, "Darling, in three weeks I have actually reduced my weight by half. Can I stay a little longer?"
"Please stay another three weeks," the husband replied.

"Honey," said the husband, "you really should do a little more dusting. I've just discovered a cobweb on your bed and thrown it into the fire."
"You dumbhead," said the wife, "that was my new nightie."

Two acquaintances met in a pub and one said to the other: "I heard you buried your wife last month."
"Yes," replied the other, "I had to... She was dead, you know."

A journalist was interviewing a successful industrialist who was celebrating his wedding anniversary. The journalist asked, "Sir, to what do you attribute your successful married life?"
The industrialist replied. "My wife and I never argue. She always goes her way and I always go hers."

"Darling," whispered a frail little husband from his chair, "I'm very sick, would you please call me a vet."
"A vet? Why do you want a vet and not a doctor?"
The husband replied, "Because I work like a horse, live like a dog, and have to sleep with a silly cow."

Wife: Honey, I'm just curious, what would you do if you came home one day and found me in bed with another man?
Husband: Oh! I'd tell him to go home and hit him on the head with his white stick.

Husband: Honey, I've insured myself for one million dollars, so should anything happen to me you will have more than enough for your maintenance.
Wife: Excellent, now we don't have to call the doctor everytime you fall sick.

A man dragged a large box up to a house and knocked on the door. A woman appeared and the man asked her, "Are you widow Smith?"
Replied the woman, "My name is Mrs. Smith, not widow Smith."
With a sad face the man said, "Wait till you see what I have in this box."

Mr.and Mrs. Henry Ford were celebrating their golden wedding anniversary when a reporter asked Mr. Ford: "To what do you attribute your successful marriage?"
Mr.Ford replied, "The formula is the same as I use in car manufacturing. I stick to one model."

Two friends met at the bar. One asked the other, "Does your wife cook best by gas or electricity?"
"I don't know," replied the other, "I have never tried cooking her."

❖

Wife: Wake up, darling, wake up.
Husband (who was fast asleep): What's the matter? What has happened?
Wife: Nothing. I just forgot to give you your sleeping pills.

❖

George knelt in front of three tombstones in tears.
"Close relatives of yours?" asked the passerby.
"Yes," said George, "this is my first wife - she died of mushroom poisoning - this is my second wife - she too died eating poisonous mushrooms."
After a brief silence, the passer-by asked, "What about the third wife?"
"She died from a fractured skull," said George. "It was her own fault - she wouldn't eat the mushrooms."

❖

A man lying on his death bed called his wife and said, "Darling, when I die, I want to be cremated."
"That would be just like you," she replied, "to go and leave your ash all over the place."

❖

There was a man who lost 90 pounds in one day. That's right, the day his wife left him.

Tom: I went out fishing with my wife this morning.
Sam: You're lucky, I'm still using worms.

A wife asked her husband to buy her a nice cool spot in the Garden of Rest for her birthday. And he did.
When her next birthday came she asked her husband what he was going to buy for her.
"Nothing dear," he replied, "you haven't used last year's present yet."

The husband came home early to find his wife is in bed, the curtains drawn and the bed in disorder.
In the wardrobe he found a jacket hanging with a man crouched below.
"Who are you?" he asked.
"I am the gas man; I have come to check the meter."
Under the bed he found another man.
"I am the electrician; I came to repair the cables."
He drew the curtains and discovered a man perched on the ledge.
"I am waiting for the bus," he said.

A married couple got a red haired child after many years. The couple had brown hair, so the husband became suspicious and the wife upset. They saw the doctor, who was puzzled, because according to the law of genetics this was not possible.

"How often do you have sex?" he asked, "Once a day, once a week, once a month?"

"No, not that often," replied the embarrassed husband.

"Aha, I get it now. Nothing to worry about, it's only rust."

❖

A woman who took her husband to the zoo. Now she goes there every Friday to see him.

❖

I know a married couple who are very happy. They have been happily married for ten years - but not to each other.

❖

Recently, in Hongkong, Mr. Robert Currie married Miss Sabina Rice. Now their friends say: "Let's us have an Indian meal with Currie and Rice."

❖

Here's some good advice for all husbands: If your wife wants to learn driving, don't stand in her way.

❖

A husband visited a marriage counsellor and said, "When we were first married, I would come home from the office, my wife would bring my slippers and our cute little dog would run around barking. Now after ten years it's all different. I come home, the dog brings the slippers and my wife runs around barking."

"Why complain?" said the counsellor, "You're still getting the same service!" .

A husband is like an old pair of shoes. They are so comfortable that you don't feel like throwing them away.

Mr. and Mrs. Thomas were known as the perfect couple with never a quarrel or a harsh word between them. When asked how they managed this, Thomas explained: "Why, it's a very simple arrangement. In the morning, she does what she wants and in the afternoon I do what she wants."

❖

"Dad, I was away for a week. Yesterday I sent a fax to my wife I'd be home that night, and when I got into my room I found my wife in another man's arms. Why, Dad? Tell me why!"

Dad kept silent for few minutes, then coolly said, "Maybe, Son, she didn't get the fax."

❖

George was weeping at his wife's funeral; but Bill, his dear friend, was completely broken up and started to cry. George consoled him: "Bill, don't take it so hard. I'll get married again soon."

❖

Hubby: Every time, after I get up in the morning and shave, I feel 10 years younger.
Wife: Then, why don't you shave before you go to bed?

❖

At a cocktail party a man was heard to complain: "Every morning, 7:30 is the worst time for me, because both my wife and the kettle start boiling."

❖

Wife (lying sick in bed): Honey, if I die, will you marry again?
Husband: Well, it's not easy to answer your question?
Wife: Why not?
Husband: You see, if I say yes - you will get angry and if I say no - she will get angry.

❖

There is this woman who calls her husband "Henry". He's the eighth.

❖

Judge: I can't understand. You look such an affectionate couple. Why do you seek a divorce?
Man: Because, your honour, we have nothing in common. I like girls and she likes boys.

A lady said, "I want some shirts for my husband, but I can't remember the collar size."
"14°, Madam?" suggested the salesman.
"That's it. How did you know?"
The salesman replied, "Well, we know that men who allow their wives to buy shirts for them are always about that size."

From her death bed, the wife called her husband and said, "One month after I die I want you to marry Miss Drone."
"Miss Drone! But she is your enemy!"
"Yes, I know that! I've suffered all these years so let her suffer now."

A wealthy man's wife was kidnapped and next morning he received a note from the kidnappers. The note said: "Either you send us one million dollars or we will send your wife back." The man was relieved that he could get away with it for so little.

"Is there evidence of any insanity in your family?" asked the doctor.
"Yes doctor," replied the woman, "my husband thinks he's the boss."

One afternoon, after a week of married bliss, the bride was enjoying a cup of coffee while the groom was absorbed in his book. Then the bride broke the silence and asked: "Darling, will you love me when I get ugly and wrinkled?"
From behind the book came the voice: "Of course I do, dear."

I met a friend who was having a walk with his wife. I remarked, "You look like a happily married couple."
"Yes," he replied with a sad face, "I am married and she is happy."

In a divorce court a woman requested the judge: "Your honour, I want to divorce my husband."
"But why?" asked the judge.
She replied, "Because he is not faithful to me."
The judge asked, "How do you know?"
She replied, "My lord, not a single child resembles him."

Two friends met. One said, "I am going overseas."
His friend asked, "Are you going for a holiday?"
"No," replied the other, "I am going with my wife."

❖

I have a husband and a vacuum cleaner. They
are both out of order.

❖

There is this man who has been drinking for one
whole week because his wife left him for good.
That's a long time to celebrate.

❖

"My wife has not spoken to me for five days. I
want to get her something to show my
appreciation."

❖

"For 20 years I have been faithful to the same
woman. If my wife ever gets to know, she'll kill
me."

❖

"My wife has just hired a good looking chauffeur. I
am beginning to get a little suspicious because
we don't have a car."

❖

<u>Car Salesman</u>: My wife is now 50. I think I'll trade her in for two 25's.

❖

"I am always kind to my wife... so she can help me with the dishes."

❖

"My wife is a woman of few words. In the morning she tells me: `Bring home some money!' and in the evening she says: `Take out the garbage!'"

❖

They are a happily married couple. They married each other for better or for worse. She couldn't find anything better - He couldn't find anything worse.

❖

A husband told his wife: "You are just like a Cadbury chocolate - half sweet and half nuts."

❖

A runner was complimented by a journalist: "You are always first in the race. What's the secret of your success?"
He replied, "Whenever I run a race I imagine that I'm being chased by my wife."

❖

A woman went to her marriage counsellor and complained, "My husband is very selfish. When he won a trip for two to Hawaii, he went twice."

"How did you get that black eye, Suzie?"
"Well, my husband came out of jail on his birthday."
"So?"
"Well, I wished him many happy returns."

Statistics show that an average woman talks 70 per cent faster than her husband listens.

"My wife has disappeared," said the man to the constable in the police station.
"How long ago?"
"5 to 6 years."
"Why did you not report it earlier?"
"Because I could not believe it."

<u>Wife:</u> Darling, may I get a new mink coat?
<u>Husband:</u> But honey, you've worn the mink coat I gave you for only a few months.
<u>Wife:</u> But you've forgotten the six years the mink wore it!

One woman told another: "My neighbour is always speaking ill of her husband. But look at me. My husband is foolish, lazy and a coward; but have I ever said anything bad about him?"

The insurance representative shook his head and said, "I'm sorry, Madam, we cannot accept your claim for your husband's death because he had no policy on his life, but carried insurance only against fire."
"I know", cried the widow, "that's why I poured kerosene over him."

Two ladies met in an ice cream parlour and one asked the other, "How do you manage to get money out of your husband so often?"
"Oh, it's simple," said the other, "I just tell him I'm going to visit my mother and he immediately hands me the fare."

During morning tea the husband said, "Well, I guess you're upset because I came home with this black eye last night."
"No, not at all," replied the wife sweetly, "you may not remember it, but when you came home you didn't have that black eye."

"Dear, if I were far away, could you love me still?"
"Of course, honey. I'm sure the farther away you are the more I would love you."

❖

Hubby: Where did you get that new dress?
Wife: Don't worry dear, it didn't cost anything. It was marked down from $200/- to $100/-. So I bought it with the $100/- I saved.

❖

It's a good thing when wives smoke. At least it gives the poor husband a chance to say a few words now and then.

❖

Husband: Darling, I'm home, and I've bought tickets for the theatre.
Wife: Oh, wonderful, I'll start dressing now.
Husband: Please do, the tickets are for tomorrow.

❖

A wife, one evening, drew her husband's attention to the couple next door and said, "Do you see that couple? How devoted they are? He kisses her every time they meet. Why don't you do that?"
"I would love to," replied the husband, "but I don't know her well enough."

Two men were chatting over their mutual friend. One said, "It's hard to believe he's in hospital. Only yesterday I saw him with a sexy blonde." The other replied, "So did his wife."

❖

We have a very happy marriage. We always give and take. She gives orders and I take them.

❖

<u>Jim:</u> Hey, Bill, why are you sitting in the front porch? Isn't it rather cold?
<u>Bill:</u> Well, yes, it is. But you see, my wife is taking her singing lessons and I don't want the neighbours to think I am beating her up.

A judge asked a man, "Why do you want a divorce after 50 years of marriage?"
The man replied, "Because I don't want to suffer all my life."

A man met his neighbour and said, "You should have drawn the bedroom curtains last night. I saw you and your wife getting into bed."
"Really?" replied the neighbour, "I wasn't home last night."

❖

Widows are happy for one good reason: they know where their husbands are.

This man was boasting: "Every night my wife takes my shoes off."
His friend asked, "You mean, when you come home?"
"No," he replied, "when I want to go out."

A man was telling his friends, "When my wife is infuriated, she starts shouting at me, my children and even at our dogs and nobody dares to answer her."
One of his friends asked, "And when you are angry, what do you do?"
The man replied, "I also shout angrily at the windows and doors of the house and none of them dares to answer back."

An overweight woman, who couldn't resist raiding the fridge between meals, decided to glue a picture of a shapely young woman to the inside of the fridge door. The reminder worked like a magic. In one month, she lost 7 pounds. Unfortunately, during the same period her husband peered inside the refrigerator so often he gained 10 pounds..!

A woman was complaining to the neighbour that her husband always came home late, no matter how she tried to stop him. "Take my advice," said the neighbour, "and do what I did. Once my husband came home at three o'clock in the morning, and from my bed I called out: `Is that you, Jim?' And that cured him."
"Cured him!" asked the woman, "but how?"
The neighbour said, "You see, his name is Bill."

Husband: It's time I got rid of our driver. He's so rash he's nearly killed me five times.
Wife: Oh, give him another chance.

Tom: I know a man who has been married for twenty five years and he spends every evening at home.
Dick: That's what I call love.
Tom: The doctor called it paralysis.

"You look troubled," I told my friend, "what's your problem?"
He replied, "I'm going to be a father."
"But that's wonderful," I said.
"What's wonderful? My wife doesn't know about it yet."

During an election in India a candidate received only three votes. When the results were published, his wife greeted him angrily.

"I always suspected there was another woman in your life. Now I know... or else you would have received only two votes."

Two friends met at a party and one asked the other for an opinion. "Tell me, Jim," he asked, "my wife is very keen to learn to drive a car - shall I let her?"

Jim replied, "Don't stand in her way!"

An armed burglar entered a house and confronted the lady. "What would you prefer to lose?" he whispered, "your money or your husband?"

The lady replied, "My husband, of course. What do you think I am, a fool?"

Hubby: You always carry my photo in your handbag to the office. Why?

Wife: When there is a problem, no matter how insurmountable, I look at your picture and the problem disappears.

Hubby: You see, how miraculous and powerful I am for you.

Wife: Yes, I see your picture and say to myself, 'What other problem can there be greater than this one?'

The husband came home and exclaimed, "I have just discovered oil on our property!"
"Oh, that's wonderful," said the wife, "now we can get a new car."
"No," said the husband "we had better get the old car fixed. That's where the oil is coming from."

A man went to the police station and said, "I want to meet the burglar who broke into my house last night." "But why?" asked the inspector.
"Well," he said, "I just want to ask him how he managed to get in without waking my wife up."

Tom: What's this knot at the hem of your shirt?
Harry: Oh, my wife tied it to remind me to post the letters.
Tom: And have you posted them?
Harry: No, she forgot to give them to me.

The difference between a mistress and a wife is ... night and day.

When a man says he had the last word in an argument with his wife - you can be <u>sure</u> it was an apology.

❖

Anniversaries

A husband and his wife had a bitter quarrel on the day of their wedding anniversary. The husband gave his wife a gift - a tombstone, with the inscription: "Here lies my wife - cold as ever." Later the furious wife bought a return present - also a tombstone - on which the inscription read: "Here lies my husband - stiff at last".

At a silver wedding anniversary the husband was standing in the corner looking very sad.
"What's the matter?" asked his friend.
"Well, a week after marriage, I got fed up and wanted to kill my wife, but my lawyer said that I would get 25 years. Now I realize that today I would have been a free man."

A couple were in bed after celebrating their golden anniversary. The wife said, "Darling, embrace me the way you used to when we first got married."
He did.
"Now dear kiss me the way you used to...   Now darling bite me the way you used to..."
At this point the husband got out of bed and the wife said, "Where are you going, dear?"
"To get my teeth," the husband replied.

During their silver anniversary, a wife reminded her husband: "Do you remember when you proposed to me, I was so overwhelmed that I didn't talk for an hour?"
The hubby replied: "Yes, honey, that was the happiest hour of my life."

A husband was absorbed in his morning papers when his wife came up and said, "Darling, remember it's our wedding anniversary. We've been married 25 years today. How shall we celebrate?"
"Oh, yes," replied the husband "we'll have 2 minutes silence."

When a bachelor marries, his wife has three qualities - she is an economist in the kitchen, an aristocrat in the living room and a devil in bed.
After a few years, sure enough the three qualities remain, but not in the same order - she is an aristocrat in the kitchen, a devil in the living room and an economist in bed.

<u>Woman:</u> I can't get my husband to remember wedding anniversaries. How about you?
<u>Friend:</u> Oh, he forgets too. So I remind him of it in March and October, and get two presents a year.

A man gave his wife an anniversary gift - beautifully packed. When she opened it, she went all to pieces - it was a time bomb.

Two friends met at the bar. One said, "You know I've worked under the same boss for 20 years." "That's nothing," replied the other, "It's our silver wedding anniversary next week."

Wedding anniversaries are very much like Martinis. After the first few, you don't bother to count them.

A man was telling his friend how he and his wife spent their silver wedding anniversary. "It was great," he said. "We flew to Bombay and went to the same Hotel where our marriage took place, ate dinner in the same corner of the same restaurant and booked the very same room where we had celebrated our first wedding night twenty five years ago. Everything was identical to what it was then - except, this time, it was I who went into the bathroom and cried."

The Newlyweds

On their wedding day, the groom said to the bride, "Honey, I love you so much I would walk through fire and water for you." The bride replied, "Make it fire. I would rather have you hot than wet."

On the first night of their marriage, the groom told the bride "Darling, love is blind."
"Yes dear," replied the bride, "but the neighbours are not, so please draw the curtains."

The bride was crying.
"What's the matter?" asked her friend.
"Well," she replied, "I didn't know until after the wedding that he had been married before and had five kids."
"That must have come as a shock to you."
"Yes, and my four children weren't happy either."

The groom tried on the shirt the bride had bought for him. "Honey," he said, "the shirt you've bought for me is too big." "Of course it is dear. I didn't want the shopkeeper to know that I had married a little shrimp like you!"

The newly married couple returned from their honeymoon. As they got off the plane at the crowded airport, the bride said, "Darling, let's make the people think we've been married a long time." "OK dear," said the husband, "then you carry the bags."

❖

The groom and the bride had their first argument. Shedding tears, the bride said, "I'm going home to my mother." The groom replied, "Good, I'll come with you, then we can both get a decent meal."

It has been noted that a lot of men lose their voice on their wedding day.

The newly weds were preparing to go out to a party. "Shall I wear my heavy brocade dress or my sheer chiffon dress, darling?" "It doesn't matter, Honey, I'll love you through thick and thin."

Soon after marriage the groom told his bride: "Honey, now that we are married, let us plan and have a clear understanding about our future together. Do you wish to be the chairman or the director?" The bride replied, "Neither; you be both. I'll just be the treasurer."

<u>Husband:</u> Honey, did you sew the button on my blue shirt?
<u>Wife:</u> No, darling. I couldn't find the button, so I just sewed up the button-hole.

40

A couple got married. The bride, being religious, hung a sign on the wall above her bed. The sign said: "I need thee everyday". A week later the groom got a sign made and hung it over his bed. The sign said: "God, give me strength".

One friend said to another: "I can easily tell you're a married man. No holes in your socks now."
"No," replied the other friend, "one of the first things my wife taught me was how to darn my own socks."

The newlywed wife looked sad. "What's the matter, honey?" asked her husband.
"I feel bad," she said, "while pressing your expensive suit I burned a big hole in your pants."
"Well, don't worry, luckily I have an extra pair of pants."
"Yes, it's a good thing you do. I used them to patch the hole."

A wife delivered a child only six months after marriage. The curious husband went to his doctor to enquire the reason. "Well, young man," said the doctor, "this happens sometimes in the case of the first child, but never afterwards."

"When I first got married," said the young lady, "I used to get so nervous that my husband couldn't sleep with me. Now, with five pegs of scotch and soda, anyone can.

"Darling," asked the bride to be, "do you think you can live on my income?"
"Of course I can, dear," said the groom to be, "but what will you live on?"

<u>Bridegroom:</u> This chicken tastes funny.
<u>Bride:</u> Well, you see, darling, it got burnt, so I put a little ointment on it.

Man at 86 who marries a girl of 25 is like buying a bestseller for others to read.

Soon after their wedding, the bride tells the groom, "Darling, now that we are married, I want you to sack your secretary."
"But honey," says the groom, "you used to be a secretary yourself."
"Yes", she replies, "that's why I want you to sack her."

Soon after the late night news on television, the groom asked the bride, "Honey, what do you think of the Middle East position?"
Said the bride, "I don't know , I've never tried it."

Only a few hours after marriage a girl went to the lawyer's office to file a divorce.
"Why", asked the surprised lawyer, "What happened in such a short time?"
The bride sobbed, "At the church, he signed his name in the register in bigger letters than mine."

"Was it a big wedding?"
"Oh, yes, it was a grand wedding. The crowd was so huge that I stood twice in the queue to kiss the bride and nobody noticed."

Bridegroom: Honey, I could sit in front of you for ever, looking into your pretty blue eyes and listening to the wash of the ocean.
Bride: That reminds me,darling, we haven't paid our laundry bill yet.

Maids

The lady of the house suspected that one of her two sons was paying too much attention to the maid. Curious, to know which one, she called the maid and asked: "Mary, suppose you could have a date with one of my two sons, which would you choose?"

"Well," replied Mary, "it's hard to say. I've had some grand times with both of them. But for real fun give me the master."

At a cocktail party, a wife was showing off her new mink coat to friends. A friend said, "It was sweet of your husband to buy you one."

The wife said, "He had no choice, I caught him kissing the maid."

The friend replied, "How terrible, I hope you sacked her?"

"No," she smiled, "I still need a new gown."

Two friends met at the supermarket and one said to the other: "Accept my heartfelt sympathy over the loss of your husband."

"Nonsense," replied the other, "he's very much at home this very moment, alive and happy."

"Yes," said her friend, "so is our maid."

A housewife came home one evening and asked her new maid, "Did you clean out the refrigerator as I told you?"

"Yes, Madam," said the maid, "and everything was delicious."

During an interview, an applicant for the post of maid made a request for a day off once a week.

"What?" replied the housewife, "a day off once a week? I don't even let my husband have that!"

A wife suspected that her husband was having an affair with the maid. She thought of a plan to take him by surprise. One Friday she told the maid to take the day off and that night she went into the maid's room, switched off all the lights and, in pitch darkness, slipped into the bed. Sure enough at midnight, there were footsteps and a figure opened the door and slipped into the maid's bed beside her. After a few passionate kisses, the wife suddenly switched on the lights and asked "Surprised"?

"I sure am, ma'am!" stammered the chauffeur.

Mother - in - Law

The wife phoned her husband in the office and said, "Darling, come home early, we are going to have mother for dinner." "Good," replied the husband, "make sure she's well done."

A man went to a drugstore and said: "I need some arsenic for my mother- in- law."
The druggist asked, "Do you have a prescription?"
"No," replied the man, "but here's her picture."

A husband and wife were shopping when the wife said, "Darling, it's my mother's birthday tomorrow. What shall we buy for her? She would like something electric." The husband replied, "How about a chair?"

The chief of cannibals invited his best friend for dinner. It turned out to be a most delicious meal. The guest thanked the host and said, "Chief, when you invite me next would you prepare the same dish again?"
The Chief replied, "That's impossible, I only have one mother-in-law."

A hunter with his wife and his mother-in-law went on safari in Africa. After some long walks in the thick jungle, the couple noticed that mother was missing. At the end of a lengthy search, they found the woman in a clearing, face to face with a lion. "Oh, what should we do?" asked the terrified wife. "Not a thing," replied the husband, "the lion got himself into this fix, now let him get himself out of it."

❖

The lawyer cabled his client overseas: "Your mother-in-law passed away in her sleep. Shall we order burial, embalming or cremation?" Back came the reply, "Take no chances - order all three."

At the funeral, a priest was consoling the bereaved man: "Come, come my good man, tears cannot restore your mother-in-law."
"Yes, I know," said the man," that's why I am crying."

Adam and Eve were the happiest and the luckiest couple in the world, because neither of them had a mother-in-law.

Two hunters met and one complained to the other, "You know yesterday, while hunting, you almost shot my mother-in-law."
The other man replied, "Oh, I am sorry. Here's my gun, have a shot at mine."

The best definition of mixed feelings is, when your mother-in-law borrows your new Rolls Royce and she drives it off the cliff.

If you want a perfect stereo for your car then let your wife sit in the front and your mother-in-law in the back.

"I like your mother-in-law more than I like mine," said the husband to his wife.
"So do I," said the wife, smiling.

Two friends met. "You look sad, Fred, what's the trouble?" asked the first friend.
"Domestic trouble."
"But you always bragged that your wife is a pearl."
"She still is. It's the mother-of-pearl that makes all the trouble."

It's nice to have a mother-in-law. Baby sitters are expensive.

Have you heard about this man who took his mother-in-law to the zoo and threw her into the crocodile pool. He is now being sued by the SPCA for being cruel to the crocodiles.

During a training examination the doctor asked one of the nurse trainees: "What would you do first if you caught rabies?"
The nurse replied: "First of all I would bite my mother-in-law."

Two neighbours were having a chat when one said, "I took my dog to the vet today because it bit my mother-in-law."
The other asked, "Did you put it to sleep?"
"No, of course not," said the first, "I had it's teeth sharpened."

This chap took his dog to the vet and asked him to cut off its tail.
The shocked vet asked, "Why do you want to do that?"
"Well," said the chap, "my mother-in-law is visiting us and I don't want any indication in our house to suggest that she's welcome."

"My mother-in-law was bitten by a mad dog in the street."
"Oh, that's terrible!"
"Yes, it was terrible to watch the dog die slowly in convulsions."

"Is it true that you just bought your mother-in-law a Jaguar?"
"That's correct."
"But you said, you didn't like her?"
"I know what I'm doing - it's bitten her twice already."

The president of the service club asked his new member, "Would you like to donate something to the home for the aged?" The new member   replied, "Yes, my mother-in-law."

The husband, surprised over the visit of his mother-in-law to his house, took his wife in the corner and said, "Did I not cable you <u>not</u> to bring your mother with you?"
"Yes," said his wife, "you did. That's what she has come to see you about."

A husband said to his wife, "Your mother has been living with us for 5 years now. Isn't it time that she got herself her own apartment?"
"My mother?" said the shocked wife, "I thought she was your mother."

Have you heard of the cannibal who got married? At the grand reception, he toasted his mother-in-law.

<u>Wife:</u> Dear, this afternoon the big clock fell off the wall. Had it fallen a moment sooner, my mother would have been hit on the head and badly hurt.
<u>Husband</u>: Oh, my God! That clock has always been slow.

Family Life

A father took his little son to the zoo. When they were walking round, the son asked, "Daddy, is it true that some animals change their fur every year?"
The father replied, "That's right son, but don't tell your mother."

There is a lot in common between the people of London and the people of Singapore. And this is very much so in family planning. In London they stop at 2 - in Singapore we also stop at 2 - but after 2:30 we carry on.

A woman went to a seamstress and ordered a maternity dress to be delivered to her by Friday. The seamstress was about to deliver the dress when she received a call from the customer already at the hospital. "Please don't bother to deliver the dress," she said, "my delivery was faster than yours."

Then there was this ten-year old child who shot both his parents and pleaded with the judge for mercy because he was an orphan.

A mother was scolding her son: "Johnny, I don't want to see you going around with that wild girl." Johnny replied, "But Mum, she is not wild at all, dad goes with her every evening."

A little boy expressed his disappointment with life. He explained, "If I'm noisy, they spank me. If I'm quiet, they take my temperature."

<u>Bill:</u> Jean, darling, quick wake up, the baby's crying.
<u>Jean:</u> It's your turn. Remember? It's half yours.
<u>Bill:</u> Yes, I know, love, but my half's not crying.

At the birthday party 2 children were boasting to each other. One said, "My father can beat your father."
The other replied, "Big deal. So can my mother."

Two ladies were having a chat. "Did you get any good wedding presents?" asked the first.
"Well, my sister promised to buy me a food mixer."
"That was sweet of her."
"No, it wasn't. When I opened the box, it was a wooden spoon."

A little boy asked his mother, "Mummy, am I descended from a monkey?"
The mother replied, "I don't know, son, I never met your father's folks."

❖

Peter enjoys two vacations a year: when his son goes to boarding school and when his wife goes to her mother.

❖

A little boy asked his father, "Daddy, can I wear my hair style like Elvis Presley?"
The father replied, "No son, you're not going to wear your hair style like Elvis Presley or any movie star."
"But daddy, you're wearing yours like Yul Brynner," said the boy.

❖

Two babies lay in a pram. One asked the other, "Are you a girl or a boy?"
"I don't know," giggled the second.
"I can tell," said the first, and he dived under the blanket, then reappeared. "You're a girl and I'm a boy."
"How did you guess?"
"Simple, you're wearing pink socks and mine are blue."

❖

Two kids were having a chat. One said, "My dad often falls asleep in the bathtub."
"But doesn't the bathtub overflow?" asked the other.
"No," said the first kid, "dad sleeps with his mouth open."

A young man won $1 million in a lottery and gave his poor parents $10/- each. The parents were shocked.
The old man said, "All these years we have looked after you and provided all your needs. Now that you are on your own, you should know that your mother and I have never married."
"What!!! Am I a ...?"
"Yes, you are and a very mean one at that."

A teenage boy approached his father and said, "Dad, would you please raise my monthly allowance by $50/-?"
Father replied, "Why, son?"
The boy said,"Well, you see, dad, these days the cost of loving has also gone up."

<u>Dad:</u> Son, what do you want for your birthday?
<u>Son:</u> Just a radio, dad, with a sports car around it.

A couple had three children. Two of them were bright, smart and handsome but the third child was dull, ugly and backward. One day the hubby got suspicious and asked, "Tell me the truth dear, is this third child really mine?"

"Yes, dear," replied the wife, "but the other two are not."

Mother: (to a naughty boy) Son, today you were very polite by not throwing the banana peel from the bus onto the road. But what did you do with it?

Boy: Oh, I simply slipped it into the pocket of the passenger sitting next to me.

One day a father called his 6 children together and asked, "Now tell me, who has been most obedient during last week and did everything mother asked?"

In one voice they all replied, "You, daddy."

Agency: What kind of a husband would you like?

Girl: One who is very romantic, a good singer and a dancer, never argues or gives trouble, doesn't drop his cigarette ash and always makes me and my mother happy.

Agency: In that case you don't need a husband; you need a TV set.

The family was browsing through their old family album when the little son asked his mother, "Mum, who is this handsome looking fellow with lovely hair?"

Mum said, "Why, that is your father!"

The son asked, "Then who is that bald headed fellow who has been staying with us all the time?"

Son: (entering the office) Hello Dad, I just came up to say Hello.

Dad: Too late my boy. Your mother came up to say Hello and took away all the change.

Preacher: (To a little boy) Do you say your prayers before you take your meals?

Little Boy: I don't have to, my mother is a good cook.

A man was telling his friend how he and his wife were coping with three toddlers without a maid.

"She sleeps with the kids while I sleep in another room. And when any night I get the urge to have her in my bed, I signal her with a whistle."

"But what if your wife got the urge, how would she indicate?" asked his curious friend.

"Well, she would softly knock on the door of my room and ask, "Darling, did you whistle?"

Young Love

She: Don't you think we should get married?
He: I'd love to, Darling, but I can't afford a home.
She: Couldn't we live with your parents?
He: That's impossible. My parents are still living with their parents.

Rich father: Well, young man, be quick and tell me the truth! Do you want to marry my daughter or do you want to borrow money?
Young man: I would prefer both, sir.

Give a girl sufficient rope and she will ring the wedding bells.

A boy approached the girl's father and asked, "Sir, can I have your daughter's hand?" The father replied, "You might as well, since you've already had the rest of her."

If love is blind then how can there be love at first sight?

It's a good thing that love is blind, otherwise it would observe too much.

One night a man parked his car and went for a walk. When he returned he found two lovebirds in the backseat of his car. He called a cop and the lovers were fined $50/- each. What shocked the owner was that he too was fined $50/- for disturbing the peace.

Isaac and Mary, in love, wanted to get married. But religion interfered. Mary was sad, so her mother suggested: "Why not sell him Catholicism?" So she sold and sold.
The date was fixed for the wedding, but one day Mary came sobbing to her mother: "The marriage is off."
"Why?"
"I think I oversold him. He now wants to become a priest."

The nervous accountant plucked up his courage, went to his employer and said, "Sir, I want to marry your daughter." "What!" said the shocked employer, "Have you seen my wife?" "Yes sir," he replied, "but I prefer your daughter."

The girl began to cry soon after the young man proposed to her. "Why the tears, love?" asked her lover. "Did I offend you?"

"No, dear," she replied, "I'm crying from great joy. Mother always says I'm such an idiot that not even a donkey would propose to me; and now one has."

❖

The girl asked her lover, "Darling, if we get engaged will you give me a ring?"

"Sure," replied her lover "what's your phone number?"

❖

<u>Girlfriend:</u> If you kiss me, it will be a feather in my cap.

<u>Boyfriend:</u> Come here and I'll make you a Red Indian chief.

❖

<u>Daughter:</u> Mummy, I don't think I can marry Bill, he does not believe in hell.

<u>Mother:</u> Don't worry, he soon will.

❖

<u>Young man:</u> Would you like to dance with me?

<u>Young woman:</u> Do you expect <u>me</u> to dance with a Baby!

<u>Young man:</u> I'm so sorry. I didn't know you were pregnant.

Of Women and Men

A woman's age is like a speedometer in a used car. We know it is set back, but we don't know how far.

A bachelor is a man who is free to choose and chooses to be free.

<u>Boy:</u> Daddy, do smart men make better husbands?
<u>Father:</u> Son, smart men don't get married.

Bachelors can't think straight. They always have curves on their minds.

Have you heard about this boy who could think of nothing but girls, girls and more girls? However, he has outgrown it. Now all he thinks of is women.

When a woman winks it means she either has something in her eye or someone in it.

The three stages of a woman are as follows: at 25 she is attentive; at 35 she is attractive; and at 45 she is adhesive.

Women always buy one size smaller to show everything. Men always buy one size larger to hide everything.

Women are always cool and calm during a crisis. A little boy ran down breathlessly to his apartment and shouted, "Mummy! Mummy! Daddy just fell off the roof!"
The mother calmly replied, "Yes I know dear, I saw him pass the window."

Men too are often cool and calm during a crisis. One fine morning the maid came running up to the master and cried, "Master, Master, your wife has just dropped dead on the floor," and the master coolly replied, "Then prepare one meal only."

A successful man is one who can earn more money than his wife can possibly spend. A successful woman is one who can find that man.

A man's life is very strange. For the first 20 years his mother keeps on asking where he is going; for another 20 years his wife asks the same thing; and at the end his creditors start wondering too.

A playboy decided to quit everything and reform. The first week he cut out cigarettes. The second week he cut out booze. The third week he cut out dames. The fourth week he cut out paper dolls.

If a man is bald at the front, he is a thinker. If he is bald at the back, he is sexy. If he is bald from front to back - he thinks he is sexy.

Wine and women are incomparable: wine improves with age.

Men make money by winking at laws; women by winking at men.

Only one man in a thousand is a leader of men. The other 999 are followers of women.

Here's good news for bald heads. "God made perfect heads. Those that were not - He covered them with hair."

❖

After God created earth, he relaxed.
After God created man, they relaxed.
But after God created woman, no one has ever had a chance to relax.

❖

A wife is a big comfort during all the troubles and problems which a bachelor never has.

❖

A woman would rather be looked over than to be overlooked.

❖

Men can't live by bread alone - they have to have credit cards as well.

❖

Worries can turn a man's hair white in one week - but vanity can turn a woman's hair any colour in one minute.

❖

Intelligence is what a man should look for in a woman after he has looked at everything else.

Every man should have a hobby - but make sure your wife doesn't know about her.

Men are impatient. They always like women to do things in a hurry - Dress and Undress.

Inspector complimenting the housewife. "Madam, it was very brave of you to attack a burglar at night when it was so dark."
"Oh," replied the woman, a little embarrassed, "to be honest, I didn't know it was a burglar. I thought it was my husband returning home late."

Wife: Darling, look I've bought a new puppy. I can't think of a nice name to give him.
Hubby: Why not give him my name, Tom or Tommy?
Wife: No, mother said that will bring a disgrace to the puppy.

School

A frustrated American school teacher resigned with remarks: "Nowadays, in public schools the teacher is afraid of the principal, principals are afraid of the superintendent, the superintendent is afraid of the school board, the board is afraid of the parents, parents are afraid of their children, children are afraid of nobody."

Johnny: Mummy, tomorrow I have an oral exam. One question the teacher will ask me is 'who made you'? What shall I say?
Mum: Say God made you.
Next day when the question came up, poor Johnny forgot what his mother had said, so he said, "Teacher, until yesterday I was sure it was my father who made me. But then mother said it was someone else - and I can't remember the name she mentioned."

Teacher: Johnny, why were you absent from school for three days?
Johnny: Sorry, teacher, my dad got burnt.
Teacher: Oh! I hope it wasn't anything serious.
Johnny: Well, teacher, they don't play games at the crematorium.

❖

A child schooling overseas wrote to his parents: "Dear Mum and Dad, I have not heard anything from you for the last three weeks. Please send me a cheque quickly so that I will know you're all right."

❖

Teacher: How did Tommy lose the fingers of his right hand?
Student: He put them in the horse's mouth to see how many teeth he had.
Teacher: So what happened?
Student: Well, the horse closed his mouth to see how many fingers Tommy had.

❖

A Sunday School teacher asked a little boy, "Johnny, where is God?"
"In the bathroom of my house," replied Johnny.
"Why do you say that?" inquired the shocked teacher.
"Because every morning my daddy pounds on the door and says: "My God, are you still there?"

Professor: Give me a good example of coincidence.
Student: My father and mother happened to get married on the same day.

The teacher, during an English lesson, asked the students: "Now tell me. What do you call a person who keeps on talking when people are no longer interested ?"
A student in the back bench replied: "A teacher."

Teacher: What were your father's last words, Johnny?
Johnny: He didn't say anything - mother was with him right to the end.

Son: Dad, I am not going to school any more. I think my teacher has gone crazy.
Dad: Why, what happened, son?
Son: Well, you see dad, the other day the teacher said 4 and 5 are 9 and this morning she said 3 and 6 are 9.

The teacher decided to test the sanity of the class.
"If a chair has 6 legs and 2 backs," asked the teacher, "how old am I?"
"You are 34", answered a bright student.
"Right, but how did you get the answer?"
"Simple, my brother is 17 and he is only half crazy."

Tommy's teacher wrote to his mother: "Tommy is a bright boy, but he spends all his time thinking about girls."
Tommy's mother wrote back to his teacher: "If you find a cure, let me know. I'm having the same trouble with his father."

There was a school girl who was so cross-eyed that when she cried, the tears from her left eye fell on her right cheek.

"I've heard your son in the university is quite an author. Does he write for money?"
"Yes, in every letter."

A Sunday School inserted a classified ad under Rummage Sale. The ad appeared as follows: "Great chance to get rid of everything not worth keeping at home but too good to throw away. Bring your husband."

Sayings

"It's a woman's business to get married as soon as possible and a man's to keep unmarried as long as possible." (George Bernard Shaw)

Benjamin Franklin said, "Every man should have a wife - preferably his own."

Oscar Wilde once said, "Men marry because they are tired. Women marry because they are curious. Both are disappointed."

Some say, "There is no life without a wife." While others say, "Wife is the knife that cuts your life."

Old Czech proverb: It's dangerous to marry a woman who looks good in black.

A mistress comes between a master and a mattress.

Bernard Shaw once said: "Marriage is like a fortress. Those who are in want to come out and those who are out want to go in."

❖

Referring to marriage, Dr. Samuel Johnson says: "No man will be fond of what forces him daily to feel inferior."

❖

In middle age, it's not the age that matters as much as the middle.

❖

A philosopher once said, "When we reach the age of thirty, we don't care what the world thinks of us. At forty we worry about what it is thinking. But at fifty we discover it wasn't thinking of us at all."

❖

A census man is one who goes from house to house increasing the population.

❖

When a man has a birthday, he takes a day off. But when a woman has one, she takes a year off.

❖

The best way to make your wife listen to you is to talk in your sleep.

When George Bernard Shaw married, someone asked him: "What do you think of marriage?"
"It's difficult to answer," he replied, "I might say it's like freemasonry. Those who are received into the order cannot talk about it, and those who are members are pledged to eternal silence."

Behind every successful man there is a woman... and she usually catches him.

It's true that money can't buy happiness; but happiness cannot buy groceries.

Be nice to people until you have made your first million bucks. After that people will be nice to you.

❖

If you hear no evil - see no evil - speak no evil - you'll never be popular at a cocktail party.

❖

They used to say, "Behind every successful man stands a woman." Now it's changed to "Behind every successful man stands a woman - and behind every woman stands a wife."

When a **diplomat** says 'yes', he means 'maybe'.
When he says 'maybe', he means 'no'.
When he says 'no', he is not a diplomat.
When a **lady** says 'no', she means 'maybe'.
When she says 'maybe', she means 'yes'.
When she says 'yes', she is not a lady.

Marriage is a romantic tale in which the hero dies in the first chapter.

DIPLOMAT: A person who remembers a woman's birthday, but never her age.

"No man will take counsel, but every man will take money; therefore, money is better than counsel."

- Swift

Banks and related issues

A Red Indian came to a bank in USA and asked for $1000 loan for three months. "We need security. How many horses, Chief?"
"Me got 100 horses."
"That's OK. Here's the money."
A month later, the Chief struck lucky in a lottery. The bank manager wired a message: "Congratulations, better deposit money in our bank for safekeeping".
The Chief wired back: "How many horses you got?"

A woman came to the bank to open a joint account. She handed the signature card bearing her and her husband's signature to the bank officer.
"Is this to be a joint account?" asked the officer.
"Right," smiled the wife, "deposit for him and checking for me."

A bank robber handed a note to a teller which said: "Put $5000/- into a paper bag. If you make a noise, I'll shoot you." The teller nodded, scribbled something on back of the note and handed it to the robber: "Straighten your tie, you stupid fool, you're on TV."

A young woman went into a bank to withdraw some money. "Can you identify yourself?" asked the bank clerk. The young woman opened her handbag, took out a mirror, looked into it and said, "Yes, it's me alright."

At a luncheon meeting a man seated next to the banker asked, "Someone told me that you were looking for a cashier?"
"Yes, we are," said the banker.
"But I thought you just hired one a month ago," said the man.
"We did," the banker said, "he's the one we are looking for."

"A banker is a fellow who lends you his umbrella when the sun is shining and wants it back the minute it begins to rain." - (Mark Twain)

Bank accounts are like toothpaste: easy to take out but hard to put back. (Robert Ackerstrom)

What is the similarity between a bank and sex? In both cases you lose interest after a withdrawal.

A shipping tycoon cashed a very large personal cheque, which came back from the bank with remarks "Insufficient funds" stamped on it's face. Beneath this stamp was another remark hand-written: "P.S. Not you ......Us."

Errand boy: Sir, now I know what's wrong with our country!
Bank executive: Oh, really and what's that?
Errand boy: Haven't you noticed, we're trying to run America with only one vice - president.

A young man was buying an apartment. He approached his bank and the officer arranged a loan for him. After completing all formalities he said to the officer, "You have been very helpful. How can I ever thank you?"
"Monthly," said the officer, "monthly."

A man went to the bank for a car loan. He asked the officer, "The sign on your desk says `Personal Loan Department'. What is a personal loan?"
The banker explained, "It's the kind of a loan where if you ever miss a payment we can get personal. And by the way, we can get very personal if you are well behind."

Based on a bank's survey, a joint current account in the bank is never overdrawn by the wife. It is simply under deposited by the husband.

When I went to the bank and applied for a travel loan, the manager turned me down. I only asked for enough money for a oneway ticket to middle east.

They say money does not grow on trees. If this is so, then why do banks have so many branches?

Put not your trust in money, but your money in trust. - (Oliver W. Holmes)

At a bankers' club meeting a reporter interviewed a banker, "What is your opinion about the business cycle during the next year?"
"I'm optimistic," said the banker, "I think next year will be the best business year the traders have ever encountered. However, I am rather worried."
"But why are you worried if you are so optimistic about the future," asked the reporter.
"Well," said the banker, "I'm afraid that my optimism may not be justified."

I have just received a statement and a letter from my bank telling me it's the last and final time they will spend twenty cents to inform me that I have five cents in my account.

A man who had borrowed heavily on his lemon grove went to see his banker. "I can't settle my note for $15,000/- due next Friday because of the heavy freeze we had last winter. I need some time."
"I can't give you an extension," the banker said, "the freeze hit everyone. You'll have to pay on Friday."
"I don't think you understand the problem," the farmer said. "Were you ever in citrus business before?"
"No" said the banker.
"Well," said the man, "starting next Friday you will be."

A very large bank in Hong Kong have their operation expanded and specialized so much, that they even have a special window only for holdups.

"Do you know I own a bank now?"
"Oh really, what is the name of your bank?"
"Piggy."

The bank manager was interviewing an applicant for the job of cashier. He called the former employer of the applicant to check his references. "We may be hiring your former employee as a cashier," the bank manager said, "I wonder if you could let me know whether he is perfectly honest." "Honest?" said the voice on the phone, "I should say he is. He has been arrested seven times for embezzlement, and each time he was found not guilty."

"My wife goes through my cheque book like a bestseller. She will not put it down until she finishes it."

A man went to the bank and approached the bank officer: "Can you tell me what a joint account is? My wife and I would like to open one." The bank officer replied, "Well, a joint account is one where the husband makes all the deposits and the wife does all the withdrawing."

The customer called his grocer and asked, "Did you get the cheque I sent you?"
The grocer replied, "Yes, I got it twice, once from you and once from the bank."

Burglars entered a bank, tied and gagged the cashier and rifled the safe. As they were about to leave, the cashier made desperate pleading sounds through the gag. Curious, one of the burglars loosened the gag. "Please!" whispered the cashier, "take the books, too. I'm $7,500/- short."

Nowadays the new drive-in banks have two windows making it easier for a husband to deposit from the front seat while his wife withdraws from the back seat.

A clever man wrote a letter to his grocer: "Send me five dozen oranges. If good, I'll send my cheque." The grocer replied: "Send your cheque, if good, we'll send the oranges."

Bankers never die. They just lose interest.

Beggar: Please, sir, may I have a coin?
Banker: I don't have any change now. I'll give it to you next time.
Beggar: Sir, it's this kind of credit that has made me a bankrupt.

A man went to the bank and applied for a loan. When his application was turned down he said, "I just talked to the wrong man. Would you please introduce me to that friendly free lending officer who appears every night in your TV commercial."

The bank received a phone call and a voice said, "Would you connect me to someone about the bonds, please."
The switchboard operator asked, "Conversion or redemption?"
"Excuse me, "said the voice, "have I called the First National Bank or the First Baptist Church?

Joint accounts prove that wives are quick on the draw.

Hubby: The bank has just returned that cheque.
Wife: Isn't that wonderful! What can we buy with it this time?

A good bank is very much like Marilyn Monroe: everything deposited in the right places.

Doctors and Patients

Man: Doctor, I want to get married. Give me a full examination.
Doctor: Sure, lets start with your head.

Speaking of doctors, a man went to his doctor and said, "Thank you, doctor, for sending my wife away on a vacation. You know how badly I need one."

A psychiatrist in his survey discovered that half of his patients went to him because they weren't married... While the other half went to him because they were.

The young woman entered the office of the psychiatrist who welcomed her and gestured towards the couch. "Do you mind if I stand," she asked, "I've just returned from my honeymoon."

There was a chronic alcoholic who visited a psychiatrist to be cured of the drinking habit. It worked well - now he can't afford to drink.

Doctor: I will examine you for $50/-.
Patient: Go ahead, Doc, if you can find it you can have it.

A woman surgeon made a complete mess of an operation she performed on a chap with heart trouble. She believed that the best way to a man's heart was through his stomach.

Have you heard of the magician who can cut a woman in half? Well last week while performing this act he had a terrible accident. Poor girl. She is now in the General Hospital - Rooms 34 and 35.

The doctor is the only man who can tell a woman to take off all her clothes and then send the bill to her husband.

The doctor jumped from the bed, got dressed and said to his wife, "Quick, get me my medical bag, some man just phoned and said he can't live without me."
"Take it easy dear," said the wife, "that call was for me."

Patient: Doc, I am having difficulty breathing.
Doctor: I can stop that.

Doctors have often ready-made sentences on their lips. For example, a nervous patient went to the doctor and said, "Doc, I often feel like killing myself. What should I do?"
The doctor replied, "Leave it to me."

Patient: Doc, I am suffering from amnesia.
Doctor: Okay, I will give you the treatment, but please pay in advance.

This blonde rang up the doctor and asked, "Doc, would you check if I left my panties behind in your examination room?"
The doctor looked around and said, "No, they are not here."
"Oh," replied the blonde, "then I must have left them at the dentist's."

Patient: Doc, my husband passed away only one year after marriage.
Doctor: Lucky man; he didn't suffer long.

Patient: Doc, do you think I will live?
Doctor: Yes, but I don't advise it.

❖

The nervous blonde sat on the dentist's chair to have her tooth extracted. Seeing so many instruments, she got frightened.
"Doc," she said, "I would rather have a baby than have my tooth pulled out."
The dentist retorted: "Well, make up your mind so that I can adjust the chair accordingly."

❖

Young model: Doctor, would you please vaccinate me where it won't show.
Doctor: All right, stick out your tongue!

❖

A psychiatrist met a friend and exclaimed, "I heard you died."
"But you see I'm alive," smiled the friend.
"Impossible," said the psychiatrist. "The man who told me is much more reliable than you."

❖

Have you heard the news about the man who swallowed a stick of dynamite. He's recovering in wards 54, 55 and 57 of the General Hospital.

❖

<u>Pretty nurse:</u> Doc, every time I check this man's pulse it runs much faster. Shall I give him a tranquillizer or a sedative?
<u>Doctor:</u> Neither, just put a blindfold on him the next time you take his pulse.

Doctors often have ready-made answers for their patients. One patient asked his doctor, "Doc, have you got anything for my liver?"
The doctor replied, "How about some onions?"

A man developed a sore throat in the middle of the night and lost his voice. As he had to give a speech at Rotary Club the next day, he got out of bed and in his pyjamas went straight to a neighbour who was a doctor. He knocked on the door, which was opened by the doctor's wife.
"Is the doctor in?" he asked in a whisper.
The doctor's wife whispered back, "No, he is not - so you can come in."

This man had an incurable cough. He tried many doctors but all in vain. Finally he saw a specialist who gave him a special mixture. Next day he died. The shocked family summoned this doctor to explain. "Well," said the doctor, "at least he has stopped coughing."

<u>Patient:</u> How about a kiss, nurse.
<u>Nurse:</u> No.
<u>Patient:</u> Please, nurse.
<u>Nurse:</u> Definitely not.
<u>Patient:</u> Come on, nurse, be a sport and kiss me.
<u>Nurse:</u> No, no, no. In fact I'm not supposed to be in bed with you.

A dentist billed a mother $40/- for pulling her small son's tooth.
"But I understand you only charge $10/- for pulling a tooth", she complained.
The dentist replied, "You're right, but your boy screamed and cried so loud that he frightened three new patients out of my waiting room."

Have you heard about the psychiatrist who has two couches in his room? They are for patients with a split personality.

A man received an invitation to an official dinner from his doctor. Unable to read the doctor's handwriting, he took it to the pharmacist, who took it inside his room, came back after ten minutes, placed a bottle of mixture in front of him and said, "That will be $20/-."

"Doctor, my son admits he has caught cholera from kissing the maid."
"Well, young people do careless things sometimes."
"Yes, but doc I've been kissing the maid myself."
"Too bad."
"And what's more, I've been kissing my wife."
"What! Oh, my God, now we'll all have it."

Doctor: We operated on your eyes and we've managed to save one of them.
Patient: Oh, thank you very much.
Doctor: Yes, we'll give it to you on your way out.

Patient: Thank you very much, Doctor, for curing my kleptomania. I don't know how to repay you.
Doctor: My fee is sufficient, however, should you have a relapse, my wife could use a toaster and a hair-dryer.

If you're poor, the doctor will cure you faster.

A doctor sent a bill to his patient. Underneath the bill he wrote: "This bill is now one year old."
Back came the reply: "Happy birthday!"

A man was injured in a terrible car accident. After two days in a coma he woke up. The surgeon standing beside his bed said, "I've bad news and good news for you. The bad news is I've cut off your good leg by mistake."

"Oh my God," said the shocked patient, "now tell me the good news fast."

"The good news - your bad leg is getting better."

Dentists are certainly luckier than lawyers or doctors. When the lawyer makes an error, his error is sometimes left hanging in the air. When the doctor makes an error he has to bury it sometimes. But when the dentist makes an error, all that he does is charge you another fee to replace it.

<u>First doctor:</u> How do you treat your patient best?
<u>Second doctor:</u> I try to kill him the same day to prevent him from dying the next day.

An elderly but modern thinking doctor gave this advice to one of his patients: "The next time you have a heavy cold, drink 6 to 7 pegs of whisky. Remember - the whisky won't cure you, but it will keep the germs too drunk to bother you so much."

A doctor, after examining a heart patient, asked, "How often do you have sex?"

The patient replied, "Every Monday, Wednesday and Friday."

The doctor suggested he cut down on this and eliminated Wednesday.

"That's not possible, Doc," said the patient, "that's my wife's day."

Woman: I'm worried. My husband thinks he's a horse.

Psychiatrist: I can cure him but it will cost a lot.

Woman: Money is no consideration. He's already made two million dollars in races.

Psychiatrist: In that case, Madam, why don't you let him run a few more races before I cure him.

A sign in the dentist's waiting room said: "Satisfaction guaranteed or your teeth refunded."

Patient (on phone): Doc, I am feeling sick. When can I come and see you ?

Doctor: How about next week?

Patient: And if I die by that time?

Doctor: Well, you can always cancel the appointment.

A patient coming round from the anaesthetic finds a doctor sitting at his bedside. The doctor says to him: "I've got bad and good news for you."

"Let me have the bad news first."

"We had to amputate both your legs just above the knees."

"Oh," groans the patient and after recovering from the shock he asks for the good news.

"Well", says the doctor, "the man in the next bed would like to buy your slippers."

Doctor: I am sorry to say the cheque you gave me last week has come back.

Patient: So has the fever, doc.

A man came to an eye specialist to get his eyes tested and asked, "Doctor, will I be able to read after wearing glasses?"

"Yes, of course," said the doctor, "why not!"

"Oh! How nice it would be," said the patient with joy, "I have been illiterate for so long."

Patient: What do you recommend a man to do when he is run down?

Doctor: He should immediately take down the number of the vehicle.

The doctor was surprised to find his nurse holding a male patient by both wrists. The doctor said, "You don't have to do that to check his pulse."
The cute nurse replied, "I'm checking his pulse while am checking his impulse."

A couple visited a clinic: "Doc, we will have sex in front of you. Can you please check whether we do it correctly?" they asked.
The doctor agreed and charged a fee of $20. The following week the same thing happened. When they came a third time, the doctor asked for an explanation.
The man explained, "If we have sex in her house, her husband will get angry. In my house, my wife will kill me. A hotel room costs $80. But you charge only $20 and I can also claim $10 from medi-save."

Inside the operation theatre the patient got nervous and said, "Doctor, I'm very much scared. It's my first operation."
The doctor replied, "I know exactly how you feel. It's my first operation too!"

A doctor can never become a successful kidnapper because nobody can read his ransom notes.

The doctor was warning his patient that he should have regular habits. The man protested: "But I do have regular habits."

The doctor asked, "Then how come I saw you with a sexy blonde at three o'clock in the morning?"

"But doc, that is one of my regular habits," said the patient.

A young blonde entered the psychiatrist's office. The psychiatrist chased her around the whole room and finally caught and threw her on his sofa. After kissing her for some time, he said, "Well, miss, that solves my problem. Now what's yours?"

A patient said to his doctor, "I see spots before my eyes."

"Don't worry," said the doctor and poured some eye drops in his eyes and asked, "Now how is your vision?"

"Ah yes, doc," replied the patient, "the spots are much clearer now."

The gynaecologist approached the nervous man in the waiting room and greeted him: "Congratulations," he said, "so you're the bouncing father? We just tried to cash your cheque!"

After a doctor had finished his lengthy speech, one man from the audience came up to him and said, "Doc, I'm glad I attended your lecture on insomnia."

"Did you find it interesting?" asked the doctor.

"No," said the man, "but it cured my insomnia."

A Japanese man went to a doctor for an eye checkup. While examining him the doctor said, "I think you have a cataract."

"No, doc," said the Japanese man, "I have a Toyota."

There was a dentist's wife who took a gun and shot her husband point blank. She shot him because she found out that he was filling the wrong cavities.

Doctor: Judging by your complaint, it appears that your sickness is hereditary.

Patient: Thank you, doc. In that case, send the bill to my grandfather.

Every time I go and visit my doctor, he makes an appointment for me to see another doctor. I sometimes wonder if he is a physician or an agent.

A doctor examined his patient and gave him six months to live. The poor man couldn't pay his bill, so he gave him another six months.

Inside the operating theatre the doctor advised the patient: "I must warn you, that this is a very delicate operation. Four out of five patients do not survive. Is there anything I can do for you before I start?"
"Yes," said the patient, "help me on with my pants."

Nowadays the new wonder drugs are very helpful to the doctors. They can keep their patients alive long enough to pay their bills.

There was a busy doctor who became so tired in his practice that he had to take two pep pills every four patients.

There was a patient who went to his doctor and said, "Doc, would you give me more of those sleeping pills you gave to my wife? She woke up again."

Patient (while browsing in the pharmacy): Do you recommend these sleeping pills?
Chemist: We certainly do, Madam, we give away a free alarm clock with every bottle.

A doctor received a phone call in the middle of the night. The voice said: "Doctor, I can't sleep. Can you help?"
The doctor replied, "Hold the phone. I'll sing you a lullaby."

A little boy asked his father, "Dad, why do doctors wear masks at operations?"
The father replied, "They have to, son; if something goes wrong, nobody can identify them."

A chap consulted a doctor because he wanted to live a long life.
"Do you smoke?" asked the doctor.
"No."
"Do you drink?"
"No."
"Do you keep late hours?"
"No."
The surprised doctor asked, "Then tell me, why do you want to live?"

Patient: Doc, give me something that will stimulate me, excite me, put me in the fighting spirit.
Doctor: Don't worry. You'll find all that in your bill.

Lady: Doctor, my husband looks at me and says I am the most beautiful woman on earth.
Doctor: Yes, I know. His eyesight is very poor.

A doctor is never happy when you're healthy.

"I have a bad headache. I'll visit the doctor."
"Nonsense, yesterday I had a headache, I dashed home, gave a big kiss to my wife and the pain disappeared. Why don't you try it?"
"Good idea, call up your wife and tell her I'll be right over."

The worried woman went to see her doctor again.
"Doctor, I can't sleep, I keep worrying I may have a baby."
The doctor reminded her, "But I gave you the pill."
"Yes, I know," said the worried woman, "but it keeps falling out."

A head nurse in the hospital received a call: "Could you tell me the condition of Mr. Smith in room 405. He was operated upon last week and I would like to know how he is."

The nurse checked the record and the chart and replied, "His condition is excellent and he seems to be making a steady improvement. Who shall I say called?"

The voice replied: "This is Mr. Smith in room 405. My doctors don't tell me a thing!"

Patient: Doc, I am worried about my future.
Doc: I'll give you a year's treatment. It'll be $500/- a month.
Patient: That takes care of your future. Now what about mine?

Patient: I have observed that you always ask your patients what they have for dinner. Why?
Doctor: Well, it's a very important question, because I bill them according to their menu.

Doctor: Don't worry about your wife. You'll have a different woman when she gets back from the hospital.
Husband: But what if my wife finds out.

A man consulted his doctor on how to commit suicide. The doctor asked, "Do you want a slow death or a fast one?"
"I don't mind a slow death."
"Then," said the doctor, "get married."

A doctor, resting in bed after a hard days work, received a phone call at night. He asked his wife to answer it and tell the patient that he was not at home but that she could advice to him. The doctor then whispered to his wife what she should say.
"Thank you very much, Mrs Brown" said the voice, "but please tell me something. Is the gentleman in bed with you fully qualified?"

Doctor: (To his friend) You see that woman sitting over there. I love her very much.
Friend: Why don't you marry her?
Doctor: I can't afford to. She is my best patient.

Patient: Do you remember giving me a plaster to get rid of my backpain.
Doctor: Yes, I do.
Patient: Well, now I need something to get rid of the plaster.

Lawyers and Judges

The judge looked at the prisoner and asked: "Have you anything to offer the court before the sentence is passed on you?"
The prisoner replied: "No, your honour, I had $100/-, but my lawyer took it."

Lawyer: I will take up your case for $20,000/-. You can pay me $5000/- now and balance at $500/- per month for 30 months.
Client: Sounds like buying a car.
Lawyer: I am.

The absent-minded judge went to the dentist and said, "Do you swear to pull the tooth, the whole tooth and nothing but the tooth?"

Judge: Did you sleep with this young woman?
Accused: No, judge, not a wink.

A woman lawyer is one who has briefs. If she doesn't have briefs, she is more probably a solicitor.

A drunkard was brought to court. Just before the trial there was a commotion in the gallery. The judge pounded the gavel on his table and shouted, "Order, order."
The drunkard immediately responded, "Thank you, your honour, I'll have a scotch and soda."

A man was sentenced to death by the electric chair. The judge, an ex-Rotarian, decided to apply the four way test here. So he asked the prisoner: "In order to be fair to you, I'll give you a choice. Would you like AC or DC current?"

A man was charged with bigamy. He was brought before a magistrate. Owing to a lack of sufficient evidence the magistrate acquitted him and said, "You can go home to your wife now."
The acquitted man replied, "Thank you, Your Honour, which one?"

A guy about to be electrocuted phoned his lawyer from the death chamber.
"They are about to make me sit in the electric chair. You are my lawyer, tell me what do I do now?"
The lawyer thought for a moment and then said, "Don't sit down."

Judge: Now tell the court exactly what passed between you and your wife during the bitter quarrel?

Defendant: Four tea cups, three saucers, two milk bottles, five tomatoes, one pot of sugar, and two pairs of shoes.

Have you heard of a lawyer who got his client a suspended sentence? That's right, they hanged him.

Client: To be frank, you are too young to conduct my case.

Young lawyer: "But sir, you can rest assured that by the time the case makes some progress, I'll be old enough.

Lawyer: Now, please tell the jury - why did you shoot your husband with a bow and arrow?

Defendant: Because I didn't want to wake the children.

First lawyer: As soon as I realised it was a crooked deal I got out of it.

Second lawyer: How much?

A visitor to a graveyard came across a tombstone with the inscription: "Here lies a lawyer and an honest man." After reading it he remarked: "The graveyard must be short of space. They have to put two in one grave."

Judge: Well, we have ten witnesses who saw you steal.
Prisoner: Maybe, your Honour, but I can give you twenty witnesses who did not see me steal it.

Lawyer: Would you please repeat the exact words the defendant used.
Witness: I'd rather not. They were not nice words to tell a gentleman.
Lawyer: Then whisper them to the judge.

A lawyer when cross examining a woman asked:
"Did you poison your husband's coffee?"
"Yes."
"Then what happened?"
"He just sat at the table and sipped his coffee silently."
"Didn't your conscience pinch you?"
"Yes it did, but only when he asked for some more."

Judge: So you say that a selfish neighbour of yours kissed you against your will?
Young lady: Yes, your Honour, he sure did.
Judge: But he is so much shorter than you. How could he reach up?
Young lady: Well, I can bend down. Can't I?

Lawyer: Ok, Mister, so you want me to defend you. Have you got the money to pay my fees?
Client: No, I haven't got any money, sir, I'm a poor man. But I've got a Fiat car.
Lawyer: Alright, you can raise money on the car to pay me . Now tell me what have they accused you of stealing?
Client: A Fiat car, sir.

A judge asked a woman witness to tell her age. "Twenty seven", she replied.
The judge replied, "You have given the same age in this court before me for many years now."
"Yes, Your Honour, I'm not one of those who says one thing today and another thing tomorrow."

Judge: Are you guilty?
Prisoner: I don't know. I haven't heard the evidence yet.

❖

A visitor in a town asked a passerby: "Do you have a criminal lawyer in town?"
The old man replied, "Well, we think so, but we can't prove it."

Judge: This is the 7th time you have appeared in the court. I fine you $100/-.
Accused: Your honour, can I get a discount for being a regular customer ?

During the courtesy campaign, the accused decided to practise politeness in the court room. On approaching the judge he said, "Good morning, your honour, how are you feeling to-day?"
The judge replied: "Fine - $100/-."

Judge: Have you ever been cross-examined before?
Accused: Many times, your honour. I'm a married man.

Judge: Have you never realized that crime does not pay?
Criminal: Yes, I have, your honour, but the hours are good.

Judge: Tell me, why did you stab your wife 47 times?

Accused: Well your honour, I didn't know how to turn off the electric knife.

❖

Accused: Your honour, I assure you I wasn't drunk. I was only drinking.

Judge: Well, in that case I will not give you one month in jail. I will give you only 30 days.

❖

Judge: Judging by your family circumstances I recommend that you seek an immediate divorce from your husband.

Lady: What! Divorce! I've spent twenty two years with that louse and now you want *me* to make *him* happy!!

❖

Judge: I've decided to award your wife $500.00 a month.

Husband: That's very generous of you, Your Honour, I'll give her $20.00 myself, too!

❖

Court scene:

1st Lawyer: You're a fool.

2nd Lawyer: And you're a damn fool.

Judge: As the learned lawyers have now identified each other, can we now proceed with the case.

❖

Secretaries

When a married man is late for dinner, either his wife is a poor cook or he has a blonde secretary.

The boss came early in the office one day and found his manager kissing his secretary. He shouted at him, "Is this what I pay you for?"
The manager replied: "No, sir, this I do free of charge."

Secretary: Boss, it's your wife on the phone. She says it's your birthday and she wants to kiss you over the phone.
Boss: Take the message, Miss Helen, and give it to me later.

At a bank meeting, the president, heated by the discussion, gets up and starts pacing up and down. The secretary notices that his flies are open, so she whispers to him, "Mr.President, the garage is open, everything can be seen."
"Ah yes, and what can you see? My new Mercedes?"
"No, a Suzuki with flat tyres."

What is the difference between a good secretary and an excellent one? A good secretary says, "Good morning, sir." And an excellent secretary says, "It's morning, sir."

❖

Some men find two women useful in their lives: a secretary to take things down and a wife to pick things up.

❖

Here is the pick of the classifieds under 'Situation Wanted': "Secretary looking for a job - no bad habits - willing to learn."

❖

Wife: Here's a bottle of hair tonic, dear.
Hubby: Oh, that's very sweet of you, honey.
Wife: Yes, give it to your secretary. Her hair is coming out rather badly on your suit.

❖

1st Secretary: Our Boss dresses so well.
2nd Secretary: Yes, and very fast too.

❖

Other Vocations

An accountant is a man who flips the sheets, makes an entry, leaves a deposit and upsets the monthly balance.

Last week we had our food in the seafood restaurant. The fish was so fresh, it was still chewing the bait.

Customer: I don't like the food here. It's terrible. Call the manager.
Waiter: Sorry sir, he's out for lunch.

Customer: Waiter, tell me, do you have frog's legs?
Waiter: No sir, it's my rheumatism that makes me walk like this.

A very rich soap manufacturer readily consented to a press interview. The reporter asked, "To what do you attribute your success?"
The soap manufacturer seriously replied, "To clean living, my dear chap, to clean living."

<u>Customer:</u> Waiter, why are you pressing your thumb on my steak?

<u>Waiter:</u> Sir, I want to make sure it doesn't fall on the floor again.

<u>Waiter:</u> Hey sir, why are you putting two spoons into your pocket?

<u>Customer:</u> Doctor's orders.

<u>Waiter:</u> What do you mean by that?

<u>Customer:</u> See what he has written on this medicine bottle; 'Take two spoons after each meal'.

A rich industrialist's wife expired. The funeral was on a grand scale and the expenditure high. He asked the chief accounts clerk to debit charges on the company's account.

"There's no heading under which the account can be debited", said the accounts clerk.

The industrialist thought for a moment: "Debit it under 'packing and forwarding' expenses!"

❖

A young accountant stayed late in the office day after day. Finally the boss asked him why. He replied, "You see, sir, my wife works too and if I get home before she does, I have to cook the dinner."

❖

Customer: Waiter, come here, I can taste soap in this food.
Waiter: That's correct, sir. It helps to wash the food down.

In a Hongkong cafe, at 3 a.m., the last guest was sleeping at his table. The cleaning woman said to the proprietor: "I've seen you shake that old fool and wake him up five times. Why don't you make him go home?"

"Nothing doing," answered the proprietor, "every time I wake him up he asks for the bill and pays it."

The other day, when I ordered a hot chocolate, the waiter brought me a Cadbury and a match.

We have a fine Chinese restaurant in Bombay. They serve you all the food you can eat for only 70 cents. The trouble is, they give you only one chopstick.

Customer: Waiter there is a fly in my soup.
Waiter: Sir, I'm afraid you will have to go in for it yourself. I can't swim.

A lady customer went to the garment shop and complained to the salesman: "You told me the sweater was 100% wool. But the label says 100% cotton."

"Madam," replied the salesman, "it is 100% wool. The label is only to drive the moths away."

Salesman: How about a pair of pyjamas for your wife?

Customer: What for, she looks better without them.

"How is business?" asked the boss.

"Fifty - fifty," replied the manager, "in the morning we get orders. In the afternoon they are cancelled."

"Waiter! Why are there coins in my soup?"

"Well, sir, remember, you said you would not come to this restaurant again unless there was some change in the meals."

The manager called his bookkeeper and asked, "Why do you go for a haircut on the company's time?" The bookkeeper replied, "Sir, because it grows on the company's time."

❖

An economist is a man who knows more about money than people who actually have it.

Do you know who invented the best cure for dandruff? Yes, it was a Frenchman . He called it the 'guillotine'.

The auctioneer asked his client, "Would you like to see a model home?" The client replied." I'd be delighted - what time does she finish work?"

Three men were in a small coffee shop. The first said, "I want a cup of mild tea."
"I'll have a cup of tea too," said the second, "but make it strong."
"Make mine tea also," said the third, "medium strong, but make sure the cup is clean."
A short while later the waiter appeared with the tray. "Which one," he asked, "gets the clean cup?"

Inspector: You've reported the disappearance of your store's cashier. Can you describe him?
Store manager: Yes, he's six feet tall and $5,000/- short.

❖

Customer: Waiter, there is only one slice of fish on my plate.
Waiter: Wait a second, sir, and I'll cut it in two.

During the shave the new novice barber asked his customer, "Excuse me, but were you wearing a red cravat when you came in?"
The customer replied "No."
"Oh, my God," said the barber, "then I must have cut your throat."

Angry boss: Again you're late this morning?
Young stenographer: I overslept.
Angry boss: You mean, you sleep at home also.

A man read an advertisement under Garage Sale: "Second hand car for only $100/-. Ideal for three." He bought the car and sure enough it was ideal for three people; one drives and two push.

"Waiter, the food that you serve in this restaurant, is it pure?"
"Yes sir, as pure as the woman of your dreams."
"Oh! Then I'd rather not dine here, thanks."

"I get two vacations a year: once when my boss goes to the States and the other when my wife goes to her mother."

A departing guest from the hotel gave a $5/- note to the porter and said, "Drink to my health."
"Thank you, sir," said the porter, "but last year you gave me $10/- for the same thing."
"That's right," said the guest, "but this year my health is better."

Customer: Waiter! Look here, this plate is all damp.
Waiter: Sir, that is your soup.

Angry boss: Why weren't you here at ten o' clock?
Late worker: Why, what happened?

A tourist at the department store went to buy bras for his wife. "We have them in African, Chinese and Russian sizes," the salesgirl said.
"That's new, what are they?" he asked.
"The African sizes uplift the fallen, the Chinese make mountains out of molehills, and the Russian suppress the masses."

<u>Diner:</u> Bring me a plate of fresh oysters. They should not be too large nor too cold. I don't want them too young or too old. And I want them right away.

<u>Waiter:</u> Yes, sir. Do you want them with or without pearls?

He changed his name to Sheraton, so it would match the name on his napkins and towels.

The post office returned the letter to the sender with the following remarks: "Dead. Address unknown."

<u>Applicant for job:</u> Just why do you want a married man to work for you rather than a bachelor?

<u>Boss:</u> Because married men don't get so upset if I yell at them.

A beggar stood in a crowded area, with a hat in each hand. A passerby stopped and dropped a coin in one hat, then asked, "What's the other hat for?"

"Business has been so good lately, that I decided to open a branch office."

Have you heard about the author who was writing a book: "A Guide for Pedestrians?" Poor author - he was run over by a bus before the book was published.

A man took a costly suit length to a tailor. The tailor measured the cloth and returning it to the customer said: "Sorry, it's not enough."

The man went to another tailor. The second tailor measured the cloth, took his measurements and said, "Come after a week."

The man went to the tailor on the appointed day and found the suit ready. While making payment, the tailor's six year old son entered the shop wearing a suit of the same cloth. The embarrassed tailor confessed the truth.

Now the man went to the first tailor and told him: "You said the cloth was not enough, but the tailor there, not only stitched a suit for me but also for his six year old son."

"Agreed, sir," said the tailor, "but my son is 19 years old."

The boss was interviewing a prospective employee. "Tell me," asked the boss, "can you take hundred words a minute?"

"Of course, I can," said the man, "I'm a married man."

❖

As the departing guest paid his hotel bill, he turned and called to the bell boy, "Quick, run up to room 220 and see if I left my suit there. Hurry, because I have only 10 minutes to catch the train."
Six minutes later the bell boy was back and out of breath. "Yes," he reported, "it's up there."

The customer was being given a shave by a new barber. After suffering several cuts on his face, he asked the barber, "Do you have another razor?"
"Yes, sir, but why?" asked the barber.
"Well," replied the customer, "I would like to defend myself."

Boss: Why didn't you deliver that message just as I told you to?
Errand boy: Sir, I did my best.
Boss: Did your best! Why, if I had known I was going to send a donkey, I would have gone myself.

At a barber's shop one colleague said to the other: "That was indeed a nasty cut you gave to that customer."
"Yes," said his colleague, "I know that. His daughter and I have a date on Saturday, and that's just to remind her."

A diplomat, engrossed in his own thoughts, entered the lift and forgot to remove his hat. There was only one fussy middle aged lady inside who asked, "Don't you take off your hat to ladies?"

The diplomat bowed a little and replied, "Only to old ladies, Madam."

❖

A customer in the restaurant called the waiter and asked for a glass of water. The waiter protested, "Sir, that's the tenth glass of water you've demanded with one cup of tea. I've never heard of anyone drinking so much water."

"Who's drinking it? My chair is on fire," snapped the customer.

❖

A man was walking in a deserted lane at night. Suddenly two men approached him. One of them said, "Sir, do you have a 10 cent coin?"

"Sure, but what do you want it for so late at night?"

"You see, there are two of us, and we want to decide by a toss of the coin who will keep your wrist watch and who your wallet".

❖

A young woman filling in a job application form wrote under "Sex": "Twice a week".

❖

The boss asked his employee why he was late for work again.

"Its not my fault, "said the man, "it's that woman's across the street. She's such a perfectionist on her dressing that when she goes skiing, she wears a complete ski outfit; when she goes jogging she wears jogging clothes; and when she leaves for work, she wears a business suit."

"So what?" asked the boss.

"Well, boss," said the employee, "today was her birthday."

❖

A customer went to a flower shop and ordered a dozen red roses to be sent to his friend who had opened a new carpet shop. At the same time he also ordered a wreath to be sent to a funeral of his friend.

The flower shop got mixed up with the order. The proprietor of the carpet shop received the wreath with the message: "With deepest sympathy". The basket of beautiful roses was delivered to the funeral bearing the message: "With best of luck in your new location."

❖

Customer (in a restaurant): How long do you expect me to wait for my half chicken?

Waiter: Well, sir, you'll have to wait until someone orders the other half. We just can't kill half a bird.

❖

A young lady politician is making house calls during an election campaign. At a doors she says, "Excuse me, I've come to request you to support me."

The man replied, "I'm sorry, Miss, you're too late. I've been married for three years."

In a crowded bus a passenger caught a man picking his pocket and said, "Aren't you ashamed to pick my pocket?"

The man replied, "Rather, sir, it is you who should be ashamed. You don't even have a cent in your pocket."

The broadcasting department in Hongkong was carrying out a house-to-house survey. In one of the houses the surveyor asked, "Sorry to disturb you, Madam, we are doing a survey. Tell me, what you think of sex on the television?"

The lady replied: "Very uncomfortable."

A young man went to a crystal gazer to have his fortune told. As he sat down, he noticed that the crystal ball had two holes in it. "What's the idea of holes?" he asked curiously.

"Well," explained the fortune teller, "on Friday nights I go bowling."

Signs

In one of the suburbs in Bombay, a sign was displayed in a small tourist hotel. It read: "The water in this hotel is completely hygienic - it has all been passed by the manager."

❖

The other day I noticed a sign outside the marriage bureau. It said, "Marry now, pay later." I wonder what it meant.

❖

Sign in a shop window: "For sale - attractive wardrobe with 5 drawers, 2 shelves and ample hanging space for a man."

❖

Due to limited parking space, the undertaker placed a notice outside his shop: "Funerals - parking for clients only."

❖

A tailor put up a sign outside his shop. 'Order your winter suit right away - because of the strong demand we will execute all customers in strict rotation'.

❖

A sign outside a French hotel said: "Customers who are not satisfied with our waitresses should contact the manageress immediately."

The tourist board placed a sign outside a nudist camp. "If you want to know what you're getting before you're married, then a visit to the nudist camp is a must."

A shop owner displayed a sign in his shop window: "My wife has been missing since last Saturday. Any one who gives any information about her, will be shot dead."

A priest, seeing a blank signboard hanging on a lamppost wrote upon it: "I pray for all."
A solicitor wrote underneath: "I plead for all."
A doctor added: "I prescribe for all."
A simple citizen wrote: "I pay for all!"

Diner: The sign in the window says this restaurant is under new management; but I see the same manager still here.
Waiter: Yes, sir, but he got married yesterday.

A restaurant-sign advertised: "Free lunch - we'll collect from your grandson."
A young man took advantage, went in, had a lavish meal and started to leave when the waiter brought the bill to him.
"Collect it from my grandson," he said smiling.
"That we will do, sir," replied the waiter, "but this bill is for the food *your* grandfather had."

❖

A crowded petrol kiosk put up a sign at the entrance, which said: "Please drive with care - you may kill our customer."

❖

A sign was placed at the entrance of the large machinery plant. It said: "Warning to young ladies: if you wear loose clothes, beware of the machinery. If you wear tight clothes, beware of the machinist."

❖

<u>Tourist:</u> This seems to be a very dangerous cliff. Why don't they put up a warning sign?
<u>Native:</u> They did put one up for three years; but no one fell over, so they removed it.

❖

Epitaph on the tombstone of a hypochondriac: "I told you I was ill".

At the Bar

Scotch is a wonderful drink. If you have a double, it will make you feel single.

A preacher walked into a saloon and ordered a glass of milk. By mistake the waiter served him milk punch. After drinking it the holy man lifted his eyes to heaven and said, "Oh lord, what a cow!"

Two friends were having a drink at the bar when one asked the other, "Tom, you look worried. What's the matter?"
His friend replied, "My secretary, my wife and my bills are overdue, all at the same time."

Jimmy, a good drinker, at a cocktail party once said, "Rewa, I only take one drink and I feel like a new man." "But then," he continued, "a new man needs a drink too."

A bartender put up a new sign at his bar: "If you are drinking to forget - then please pay in advance."

The drunkard was brought to the police station.
He asked, "Why have I been brought here?"
The police inspector said, "You've been brought in for drinking."
"Well," asked the drunkard, "when do we start?"

Two men were having a drink at the bar when they struck up a conversation.
"I will never forget the day I fought a lion single-handed."
"How did you come out?"
"Single handed!"

Two men were having a drink in the bar when one asked the other: "At home are you a man or a mouse?"
"I'm a man."
"How do you know?"
"Because my wife is afraid of mice."

Two men struck up a conversation in a bar.
The first said, "I was hypnotised last week."
"What does hypnotised mean?" asked the second.
"Well, to hypnotise is to get the man in your power and make him do whatever you want."
"That's not hypnotism, that is marriage."

"You're a real chain smoker - using one cigarette to light the next. You are simply wasting a lot of money that way."
"But you don`t know how much I am saving on matches."

A social worker approached the lady of the house and asked, "Madam, would you like to donate something for the home of the chronic alcoholics?" The lady of the house replied, "I certainly would. Please, wait till the bar closes and I'll give you my husband."

A drunkard was staggering in the park when he came across a man doing press-ups. Shakily he bent down and said: "Excuse me, sir, I think someone has stolen your girl."

A man nervously rushed into a bar and asked: "Does anyone here own a black dog with a white collar?" There was no reply. Raising his voice, he asked again. And once again no one responded. "Oh my God," whispered the man, "I must have run over the vicar."

Club Life

At a club's convention in Bangkok, a survey was conducted during a fellowship gathering in which two questions were asked. "After sex do men sleep on the right hand side or left hand side of the bed? And what percentage." The result of the survey showed that 5 % sleep on the right hand side of the bed, another 5 % sleep on the left hand side of the bed and the balance of 90 % get up and go home.

Two strawberries met in a jar. One said to the other, "You know, if only we had not met, we would not be in this jam."

After the induction of a Scotsman in the service club, the president requested him for a donation to the local orphanage. Promptly the Scotsman sent two orphans.

A mother took her little girl to the zoo. They came across a cage with two lions: a male and a female. The girl asked, "Mummy, how do lions make love?" Mother replied, "I don't know, dear, I married a Rotarian."

At a dinner party, the speaker who was a guest of honour, was about to deliver his speech when his wife sitting at the other end of the table, sent him a note with the word 'KISS' scribbled on it.

A guest seated next to speaker said, "Your wife has sent you a KISS before you begin your speech. She loves you very much."

The speaker replied, "You don't know my wife. Here the letters K-I-S-S stand for `Keep It Short, Stupid'."

An International President of a social club makes a visit to another town in his district. The prominent members of the club take him to see a new zoo. They come to a spot where they see a lion and a goat together in the same cage. Pointing the cage to the prominent gathering he says, "Here is a perfect example of peaceful co-existence, which I always preach."

He than asks the zoo keeper standing beside the cage, "Tell me, how do you manage this?"

"Well, it's very simple, sir," says the keeper, "I put in a new goat everyday."

A guest speaker at an evening meeting asked the club president : "How long can I speak?"

"Speak as long as you like," said the president, "but we all go home at 8 o'clock."

At a social club fellowship-cum-meeting in India, a band was invited to play. During the meeting the president announced: "Now there will be a collection for charity. Those who volunteer to donate Rs. 50/- please stand."

Not a single one responded, so the President called on the band to play the National Anthem. Everybody stood up and the total collection was Rs. 6 000/-.

An aged speaker felt uneasy during a Rotary lunch. The chap seated next to him asked him: "What's the problem?"

"Well, I've forgotten my dentures, and I'm embarrassed to speak."

"No problem, I've 5 or 6 sets of teeth in my pocket. Use one which fits you well."

The old man tried them all, found a set that fit and was delighted.

"Are you a dentist?" he asked.

"No, I'm an undertaker."

After a Rotary lunch meeting, two members were waiting for their cars when one said to the other: "Did you hear Tom snoring at our table while the speaker was giving a speech? Isn't that awful?"

The other replied: "Yes, I heard him. He woke me up."

A man was hunting for the first time. Full of excitement he returned to the lodge and boasted loudly, "I've killed a lion, I've killed a lion."
One of his friends who knew he couldn't tell a lion from a tiger asked, "How do you know it was a lion?"
"Very simple, I found a membership card in his pocket."

At the toastmaster's club a member was heard complaining: "I will never become a good speaker. The moment I open my mouth, my wife interrupts."

A dying club member told his wife, "I want my fellow club members to be my pall bearers."
"Why?" she asked, "you never attended meetings regularly or took an active part in the club."
"They have carried me this far," he replied, "they might as well carry me the rest of the way."

Wife: You delivered an excellent speech.
Hubby: Thanks, dear, but the audience was full of fools and idiots.
Wife: Is that why you addressed them as your brothers and sisters?

The after dinner speaker looked to his right - the crowd on the left disappeared; he looked to his left - the crowd on the right disappeared. Only one man stood waiting. The speaker said, "Thank you for waiting. You must be enjoying my speech."
"Well, sir, I'm waiting to pick up my little carpet on which you are standing."

At a Rotary convention a delegate was asked in an interview why he never took his wife with him whenever he attended. He replied, "I have two reasons. It's half the cost - and twice the fun."

After a dinner speech, the speaker scolded his secretary: "Why did you write such a long speech for me? You saw how people were feeling bored!"
The secretary replied, "Sir, it wasn't a lengthy speech at all; but I did make one mistake - I gave you all three copies of the speech."

A speaker gave a talk. After the lecture he invited the audience for questions to be submitted on slips of paper. A slip came on which was scribbled "ASS". The speaker, with a smile, showed the slip to the audience and said, "the sender has written his name but not the question."

<u>Toast:</u> Let's all drink to our wives and girlfriends. May they never meet.

❖

A Rotary visitor to Japan told a joke lasting two minutes. The interpreter then translated using only few words. Everyone laughed. Afterwards the visitor asked the interpreter how he translated such a long joke so quickly. "Well, I didn't think they would get the point, so I said, "'Our guest has just told a joke. Everyone please laugh.'"

❖

The president made an announcement: "We've decided to let members bring their wives to one luncheon meeting a month."
A member replied, "But I'm not married. Can I bring a girlfriend?"
The president said, "I suppose it's all right, provided she is the wife of a member."

❖

At the luncheon meeting, the speaker seated next to Kitty was boasting: "When I talk, people listen with their mouths open."
"Ah," said Kitty, "you must be a dentist."

❖

Church

At a church wedding a little boy asked his father: "Daddy, why do they rope off the aisles at a wedding?" The father replied "Son, this is to make sure that the groom can't get away."

Once I attended a church wedding. At the altar stood the bride and the groom looking at each other with love and affection. The bride said: "My little peach." The groom said: "My sweet melon." The preacher said: "I now pronounce you `fruit salad'."

At a church wedding little junior asked his father, "Dad, why don't they give the groom a shower?" The father replied, "Son, that is because he'll be in hot water very soon!"

A pretty woman was about to enter church in a topless dress, when the vicar said, "I'm sorry, Madam, but I cannot allow you to enter church like that."
"But I have a divine right," protested the woman.
"Yes," agreed the vicar, "and you have a divine left too, but I still cannot."

During a sermon the priest thought of an example to tell the congregation the difference between 'knowledge' and 'faith'. "In our midst," he said, "we have Mr. Sam with his wife and 2 children. Now, she knows they are her children - that's knowledge. He believes they are his children - that's faith."

Married man: Father, during your service, you said it was wrong for people to profit from other people's mistakes. Did you really mean it?
Preacher: Of course I did.
Married man: In that case please refund me the $50/- I paid you for marrying me to my wife 10 years ago.

Priest (to an old man on his death bed): Have you made your peace with God?
Old man: I don't think we have quarrelled even once in my eighty years of life.

Mother: Julie, did you behave well today at the church?
Julie: Yes, Mum. A man offered me a big plate of money, and I said, 'No thank you'.

Referring to a priest, a little boy remarked, "I don't know, why they call him `Father', when he is neither married nor has any children."

❖

The priest carried a pocket phone wherever he went. One day he was invited by two elderly women who asked him to pray for them. As soon as the priest finished his prayer for them, the phone in his pocket started ringing. The women looked startled and one of them said, "I've never known a priest with such direct immediate contact."

❖

Priest: You may not know, but every night I pray for you.
Blonde: Well, you don't have to - I am on the phone.

❖

Before retiring to bed on his wedding night, the young priest turned to his bride and said "Excuse me dear, I am going to pray for guidance."
"Darling," said his wife, "I'll take care of your guidance. You pray for endurance."

❖

Preacher: (To a car mechanic) Please be easy on my car repair bill. You know I am a poor preacher.
Mechanic: Yes I know, I heard you on Sunday.

❖

At the Pearly Gates

A priest and a permanently drunken bus driver from the same village arrive at the pearly gates and both request entry to heaven. Says St. Peter to the priest, "You wait two years," and to the bus driver, "You go straight in."

The priest protests, "How come? I have been preaching every Sunday for so many years - and he is nothing but a drunken bus driver."

St. Peter replies, "Listen, when you preached, they all slept, but when he drove, they all prayed like crazy."

Two friends arrive at the pearly gates. St. Peter asked, "Tell me the truth, have you all been faithful to your wife?"

"Yes," says the first friend.

"You get a Rolls Royce and are admitted to heaven."

The second friend says, "I was a salesman, during my travels I was unfaithful over 200 times."

"At least you're honest, you get a skateboard and admission to heaven."

Later the second man meets the first man in the Rolls, who is very sad. "Why are you sad?" asks the second man.

"I just saw my wife on a skateboard," replies the first.

A man said to St. Peter, "I want to see what hell is like." He saw a big gathering, having a big feast with a big variety of food. Returning to heaven he had dinner with St. Peter and only one dish was served. Surprised he asked, "Why only one dish?" St. Peter replied: "It's a hell of a problem cooking for two."

❖

Five frogs came to the pearly gates. St. Peter turned to the first frog and said, "What have you been doing down below?"
"Going in and out of puddles."
St. Peter admits the frog to heaven and asked the same question of the second, third and fourth frog, all giving the same reply and all are admitted to heaven.
The fifth frog, a very pretty one, was asked her name. "My name is Puddles," she replied.

❖

Two friends come to the pearly gates. "How did you die?" asked one.
"Frozen to death. And you?"
"I suspected my wife was having an affair, went home early, looked all over - inside the cupboards - under the bed - behind the curtains - and the strain caused a heart attack."
"You stupid fool, why didn't you look in the fridge. You would have saved my life and yours."

Among the Nations

When an Englishman can't get along with his wife, he goes to his club. A Frenchman goes to his mistress. The American goes to his lawyer. And the Singaporean will simply go to the soccer game and roar.

A married woman should adopt four personalities to be a perfect wife. In the morning, she should become English - no talk, no chatter, but silence because the husband is busy thinking of business. In the afternoon she should become Scandinavian - she should serve the most delicious and beautifully presented lunch - because the way to win a man's heart is through his stomach. In the evening she should become an Italian - she can talk as long as she likes as the husband has plenty of time to listen. At night she should become French - this needs no explanation.

On the first day of their marriage a Scotsman took his bride to a very posh restaurant. As they sat down, the Scotsman said to her, "Darling, now that we are married, you and I both make one." The bride replied, "Yes dear, but please order lunch for two."

A Scotsman went into the pro shop and asked the pro: "Could you put my name on this ball?" The pro did so. "Could you also put MD after it. I'm a doctor." The pro obeyed. "There's just one more thing," went on the Scot, "can you squeeze `hrs 10 to 4' on it as well?"

There was this Scotsman who was wearing a black band on his sleeve while playing golf. He was in mourning for the golf ball he had lost.

Three partners, a communist, a socialist and a capitalist, joined hands in a mining venture and made US$150 million profit. The communist partner filed a tax return, declared all income, claimed all deductions and paid all profits to the government. The socialist partner filed his tax return, paid all profits and retained 10% for research and development. The capitalist partner filed a tax return, declared all his income, claimed all the deductions and applied for a refund.

There was this Scotsman who fired a gunshot on Christmas Eve from the rooftop of his house, then came downstairs and told his kids that Father Christmas had committed suicide.

France is beautiful. A friend of mine, when he was in Paris, saw some really beautiful things in a shop. He even followed one of them home.

Sometimes it gets extremely cold in Scotland. During one such winter, a snowman was seen making a little boy.

A group of Australian tourists was being guided through an ancient palace in India. The guide explained, "This place is 500 years old. Not a stone in it has been touched, nothing altered, nothing changed or replaced in all those years."
"Well," said one woman dryly, "they must have the same landlord as I have."

France is beautiful. But one day I was stung in Paris. I was sold a ticket to see the 'best leg show in France'. It turned out to be a 5-day bicycle race.

The French found out why their flights were delayed for departure. So they placed a signboard outside the Paris airport: 'Please start kissing ahead of time so that planes can leave on schedule.'

The French have invented a new gadget to improve flights. If you press a button on your seat, out comes the belt. Press the button on the belt and out comes the pillow. If you press the button on the pillow, out comes a hostess. If you press the button on the hostess, out come your teeth.

Three women entered a lingerie store. The American said, "I want seven pairs of panties - one for every day of the week."
The French woman said, "I want five pairs for Monday to Friday. Because weekends I spend with a lover and don't need to wear any."
The Russian woman said, "I want 12 pairs of panties for January, February, March...

The French are very slow at love making compared to Americans. A French man takes his time. He first kisses the finger tips; then kisses the hand; then the elbow; then he kisses the shoulder and then kisses the back of the neck. By that time the American man is already back from his honeymoon.

Did you know that there is a village in Thailand where the population has remained the same for the past 30 years? Every time a baby is born a man leaves town.

A Chinese delegation visited America. At a tea party hot dogs were served. During a toast the US diplomat said, "We hope you like our popular hot dogs."

The Chinese diplomat also raised a toast and replied, "We like your hot dog. In China we also eat hot dog, but we don't eat the part the Americans eat."

A Scotsman was seen driving a new Cadillac.

His friend said, "How did you get this?"

The Scotsman replied, "I was having a walk when a beautiful blonde offered to give me a lift. She drove to a lonely spot, stopped the car, got down, undressed herself and said, `Take what you want'- so I took the car."

An Englishman, a Frenchman and a Russian were debating the origin of Adam and Eve. Said the Englishman, "They must have been English, since Adam was polite by offering the only apple to Eve."

The Frenchman protested, "I say they were French because Adam gave the only apple to Eve to seduce her."

"They must have been Russian," said the Russian, "Because they had no clothes to wear, only one apple to share and they still thought they were in Paradise."

An Englishman and a Scotsman wanted to fulfil the last wish of their dear departed friend who, on his death bed, had requested them to put 10 pounds each in his coffin. The Englishman put in a 10 pound note. The Scotsman took out this 10 pound note and put in a cash cheque for 20 pounds. A week later the Scotsman was shocked to learn that the cheque had been presented and cashed. The undertaker was an Irishman.

❖

A Scot was about to remarry. A friend reminded him, "Your first wife swore she would crawl out of grave and haunt you if you ever touched another woman."
"That's right," agreed the Scot.
"Aren't you scared?"
"No, no,- she'll have a long crawl... You see, I buried her upside-down."

❖

An English diplomat, whose son had just graduated, was worried about his direction in the future. So one day he placed a bible, a ten pound note and a glass of beer on the table and hid behind the curtains. The boy came in, put the bible in one pocket, the ten pounds in another, drank the beer and left the room.
"My God," said the diplomat, "the boy is really stepping into my shoes."

When you tell a joke to a German, he laughs once because everybody is laughing. An Englishman laughs twice: once to be polite and again in the middle of the night when he gets it.

Scotsman: Honey, it's our silver anniversary and I have a surprise for you!
Wife: Yes?
Scotsman (holding her hand): You see this engagement ring I gave you 25 years ago. Well, I just paid my final installment to-day and now I'm proud to say it's yours!

A Texan had three swimming pools in his mansion. When asked why, he said, "One pool has warm water to swim in the winter, the other cold water for swimming in the summer."
"And why the 3rd empty pool," asked the guest.
"Ah! That's for people who can't swim."

A Texan visited Germany. He was asked to describe his farm. So he started: "When we drive around the farm, it takes almost a full day."
"Oh yes," said one of the listeners, "after the war we also had a car like that."

Golf

The wife, upset over her husband who spent all his time playing golf, said, "You think so much of your darn golf game that I'm sure you don't even remember the day we were married!"
The husband replied, "Of course I do, dear. That's the day I sank a 50 foot putt."

A golfer hired a caddie for his tournament game. This caddie turned out to have hiccups all day. On the last hole the golfer had to sink a one foot putt to win the tournament. He lined up the putt carefully, addressed the ball and missed. He turned to the caddie and said, "See, what you made me do. You and your hiccups."
"But I didn't hiccup," protested the caddie.
"I know," said the golfer, "but I allowed for it."

The nurse was asking her colleague: "Who are they operating on?"
"Oh, it's some guy who had a golf ball knocked down his throat."
"And who is the poor old chap waiting outside? Is it his father?"
"No, that's a golfer. He is waiting to get on with his game."

Two golfers were putting on the green when a funeral procession appeared on the main road. As the cortege passed, one golfer removed his hat and held it over his heart.

"That was very decent of you. Do you know the deceased?"

"Yes," said the first golfer, "she is my wife."

During a trial the judge asked the accused, "Tell me, how did the trouble start?"

The accused replied, "Well, your honour, she asked me to play around and I didn't know she was a golfer."

A lady went to her lawyer and said, "I want to divorce my husband. I haven't seen him for 11 years."

"Have patience," said the lawyer, "maybe he has taken up golf."

The golfer called one of the caddies and said, "I'm playing for the cup and I want a caddie who can count and keep the score. What's 3 and 5 and 4 come to?"

"11, sir," said the caddie.

"Good, you'll do perfectly," said the golfer.

During a round of golf the golfer asked: "Caddie, why are you looking at your watch so often?"
The caddie replied: "It's not a watch, sir, it's a compass."

❖

This golfer returned home with a sad face.

His wife asked: "You had a poor score?"

"No, not bad, I played 83."

"Did you and Peter have an argument?" she asked again.

"No," he replied.

"Well something must have gone wrong."

"Yes, as a matter of fact it did. While playing, Peter dropped dead on the 14th hole."

"Oh, no!" gasped the wife, "No wonder you're upset."

"Yeah, from then on, it was just shoot and drag Peter, shoot and drag Peter...."

The shocked golfer rushed into the club house crying that he had just killed his wife. "I didn't know she was behind me," he sobbed, "I started my backswing and the club hit her head and she was dead before she hit the ground."

"What club were you using?" asked the other golfer.

"Number Three Iron."

"Oh, oh, that's the club that always gets me in trouble too."

"My wife has given me a choice. Either I sell my golf clubs or we get a divorce... I am going to miss her."

After paring several holes, the golfer asked his regular caddie, "Notice any improvement to-day?" The caddie replied, "Yes, you've had your hair cut, sir."

A golfer brought a guest on the golf course for a game. The guest placed the ball on the tee, took a swing and completely missed the ball. He took a second swing and again he missed. On the third swing he duffed and the ball trickled 20 yards off the tee. The guest looked at the host and said, "You know something; this is a difficult course."

A beginner golfer at a short par three hole took a full swing and whacked the ball. The ball hit a rock, bounced off and hit a tree, then it ricochetted and hit another tree and finally landed on the green about two inches from the hole. Greatly disappointed he said, "If only I had hit it just a wee bit harder."

After an enjoyable round of 18 holes, one golfer asked the other: "Shall we have another game on Friday?"
The second golfer replied: "Well, I was going to get married on Friday.... but I can put it off."

Flying

A US single-seater plane crashed in Russia. The severely injured American pilot was warded in a hospital in Moscow. The Russian surgeon said, "Your right leg is bad, it has to be amputated."

The pilot replied, "OK, but please send it to my home town in California."

The surgeon agreed, but two days later the same thing happened when the left leg was amputated; and again when the right arm was cut off. Every time the pilot made the same request to send the limb to his home town in California.

Finally, a week later the surgeon once again came with the bad news and said, "Your left arm is also badly affected. It needs to be cut off too, but please don't make the same request again."

"Why not?" asked the pilot.

"Because," replied the surgeon, "the Russians think you're trying to escape."

Every Year it takes less and less time to fly to Asia and more and more time to drive to office.

In this jet age you can have breakfast in London, lunch in New York, dinner in San Francisco - and your baggage in Mexico.

A pilot went for a medical checkup. After a full examination the doctor asked the pilot, "When did you last have sex?"
The pilot replied "1955."
"Why so long ago?" asked the doctor.
The pilot replied, "That's not so long ago. It's only 21:45 now."

A bearded man slipped into the cockpit, pointed a gun at the pilot and whispered, "Take me to Paris."
The pilot replied, "But we're supposed to be going to Paris, anyway."
"I know", said the bearded man, "but I've been hijacked to Liberia twice before, so this time I'm not taking any chances."

The worried pilot made an urgent call to the control tower, "I'm out of fuel 500 miles over the Indian ocean - urgently request instructions."
Back came the reply from the control tower: "Repeat after me - 'Our Father, who art in heaven, hallowed be thy.... ' "

Very soon it will take only two hours to get around the world. One hour for the flight and one hour to get to the airport.

Three passengers were in the plane; Reagan, Gorbachev and Marcos. The plane was loosing height and they only had one parachute. Reagan said, "Let me use it, I'm the leader of the free world." Gorbachev said, "Let me... I'm the leader of new wave." Marcos proposed: "Let's put it to vote." All agreed. Marcos won 14 to 2.

Has any one ever complained of a parachute not opening?

"I would be scared to be up there in a plane."
"I would be scared to be up there without one."

<u>Passenger:</u> This flight is very bumpy.
<u>Hostess:</u> But, sir, we are still parked in the holding bay.

A passenger seated in a plane by the window, was enjoying the beautiful clouds passing by when suddenly a parachutist appeared in front of his window. "Hello there, would you like to join me?" asked the parachutist. "No thanks," replied the passenger," I am happy where I am."
"Suit yourself, I am the pilot."

Military

A Japanese general and a US major were chatting. The Japanese general said: "How come you always win your battles but we always lose ours?"
The US major replied: "Because we always pray to God before we go into battle."
"We also pray to God, but we never win."
"Ah yes!" retorted the US major, "but not everyone can understand Japanese."

<u>Army patient:</u>Doctor, everyday you probe my wound. You don't know, how much it hurts.
<u>Doctor:</u> Well, I must try to find the bullet.
<u>Army Patient:</u> What! Why didn't you say so. I have had it in my pocket all the time.

A pretty blonde who joined the army was asked by the captain, how she liked military life.
She summed it up, "It's like this, `Yes - Sir', all day and `No - Sir', all night."

A young soldier was awarded a gold medal for saving three women in the war... One for his major, one for his general, and one for himself.

Tax

A taxpayer sent a short note to the tax department, saying that 12 years ago he had cheated on his income tax and he had not been able to sleep since then. He enclosed $100/- and added: "If I'm still unable to sleep, I will send the balance."

❖

An entrepreneur lay on his death bed and requested that his remains be cremated. His friend agreed and asked what was to be done with his ashes.

"Put the ashes in an envelope," said the dying man, "mail them to the tax department and tell them that now they have everything."

❖

<u>Tax inspector:</u> You should pay your tax with a smile.

<u>Blonde:</u> I have tried several times, but everytime you insist on cash".

❖

A new businessman was filling in his income-tax return when he came across the column: "Exemption claimed for children". Under this column he wrote in capital letters: "COMING ATTRACTION - WATCH THIS SPACE IN NEXT RETURN."

❖

Film

The most healthy and happy women in the world are in Hollywood, because they sleep under the stars every night.

An actor married an actress. After the marriage ceremony, the groom asked the bride, "Darling, what is your greatest desire?"
The bride replied, "I wish to have shorter honeymoons, but plenty of them."

Reporter: I am sorry I couldn't be present at your latest wedding.
Film actress: Don't worry. You can come to the next one.

And here's what one actress says: "I have played a maid in so many movies that when I return home from work at night, I go through the back door."

"Did that new play have a happy ending?"
"Oh yes, everybody was glad it was over."

During the shooting of a movie, the director said, "Jack, come on, jump now."

"But, sir, from this fifth storey? I'll be killed!" protested Jack.

"Oh, don't worry," said the director, "it's the last scene in our picture."

Friend: There's a bishop waiting outside to meet you. He said he married you sometime ago.

Film Actress: Gosh! I am quite certain I never married a bishop.

Handsome Man: I would very much like to marry you some day.

Film Actress: Fine, I'll put you on my wedding list.

Friend: (To a new actor) Is your first picture a comedy or tragedy?

New Actor: Well, if enought tickets are sold, it's a comedy. Otherwise it's a tragedy.

Animals

John: I have an unusual dog. It has no tail.
Harry: So I noticed, so how do you know when it's happy?
John: When it stops biting me.

"Hello, police? I've lost my parrot."
"Sorry, Madam, that's not our job."
"But my bird is very intelligent and can talk in three languages."
"Well, in that case you'd better hang up, Madam, he may be calling you right now."

A man read in a health magazine that nicotine in cigarettes caused lung and throat cancer in rats and mice. So now, as a precaution, he puts all his cigarettes safe inside his steel cabinet where the rats and mice cannot get at them.

A man finally bought a parrot at an auction after some very strong bidding. "I suppose the bird talks?" he said to the auctioneer.
"Talk?" came the reply. "He's been bidding against you for the past half hour!"

Horses are more sensible than men. When ten horses run, thousands of people will go and watch them. But when ten people run, not even one horse will go and watch.

Boarder: I don't like all those mice in my room.
Landlady: Well, keep those you like and chase out the rest.

A man had three cute puppies which he named: "Sherry, Brandy and Shandy". One day he had a visitor. The host introduced his three little puppies to him: "This is Sherry, Brandy and Shandy."
"No, thank you," said the visitor, "I'll just have a scotch and soda."

A horse is the only animal which can take several thousand people for a ride at the same time.

Husband: Darling, I don't think you can ever train that dog to obey you.
Wife: Nonsense Dear, remember how stubborn you were when we first got married.